ADVANCED TOPICS
IN SCIENCE AND TECHNOLOGY IN CHINA

ADVANCED TOPICS
IN SCIENCE AND TECHNOLOGY IN CHINA

Zhejiang University is one of the leading universities in China. In Advanced Topics in Science and Technology in China, Zhejiang University Press and Springer jointly publish monographs by Chinese scholars and professors, as well as invited authors and editors from abroad who are outstanding experts and scholars in their fields. This series will be of interest to researchers, lecturers, and graduate students alike.

Advanced Topics in Science and Technology in China aims to present the latest and most cutting-edge theories, techniques, and methodologies in various research areas in China. It covers all disciplines in the fields of natural science and technology, including but not limited to, computer science, materials science, life sciences, engineering, environmental sciences, mathematics, and physics.

For further volumes:
http://www.springer.com/series/7887

Zibin Zheng • Michael R. Lyu

QoS Management of Web Services

With 42 Figures

Zibin Zheng
The Chinese University of Hong Kong
Hong Kong
People's Republic of China

Michael R. Lyu
The Chinese University of Hong Kong
Hong Kong
People's Republic of China

ISSN 1995-6819   ISSN 1995-6827 (electronic)
ISBN 978-3-642-44271-1   ISBN 978-3-642-34207-3 (eBook)
DOI 10.1007/978-3-642-34207-3
Springer Heidelberg New York Dordrecht London

Preface

Web services are widely employed for building loosely coupled distributed systems, such as e-commerce, e-government, automotive systems, and multimedia services. Quality of service (QoS) is usually engaged for describing the nonfunctional characteristics of Web services. QoS management of Web services refers to the activities in QoS specification, evaluation, prediction, aggregation, and control of resources to meet end-to-end user and application requirements. This book delivers the main contemporary themes in service computing, including service QoS evaluation, service QoS prediction, and QoS-based service fault tolerance. To collect sufficient Web service QoS data, an effective and efficient Web service evaluation mechanism is required. However, in the real world, a comprehensive Web service evaluation may not be possible. Therefore, Web service QoS prediction approaches, which require no additional real-world Web service invocations, are becoming more and more attractive. Finally, employing the Web service QoS values, QoS-aware fault-tolerant service-oriented systems can be built using redundant Web services on the Internet. Dynamic selection and reconfiguration of the optimal fault tolerance strategy becomes a necessity in service computing.

Different from the previous books, this book not only provides researchers with the latest research results timely and extensively but also presents a comprehensive overview of the QoS of Web services. Specifically, a new theme of service evaluation, service prediction, and fault-tolerant Web services goes through the whole book, making various machine learning models understandable and applicable to a large proportion of the audience, including researchers in service computing, practitioners in service-oriented architecture (SOA), and graduate students in systems, software, and service engineering.

Shenzhen Research Institute   Zibin Zheng
Department of Computer Science and Engineering   Michael R. Lyu
The Chinese University of Hong Kong
20th November 2011

Acknowledgements

Both authors would like to acknowledge the invaluable cooperation of many collaborators who have been involved in the research projects in the past few years. These projects served as a basis for some key research findings that underlie several of the ideas discussed in this book.

In particular, we would like to send special thanks to Prof. Kam-Wing Ng, Prof. Man Hon Wong, Prof. Irwin King, Prof. Shing-Chi Cheung, Prof. Jie Xu, Prof. Lui Sha, Prof. Xicheng Lu, Prof. Huaimin Wang, and Prof. Ji Wang for their invaluable encouragement and advice over the years. We would also like to send our sincere appreciation to our group members: Xinyu Chen, Xiaoqi Li, Yangfan Zhou, Jianke Zhu, Hao Ma, Hongbo Deng, Haiqin Yang, Wujie Zheng, Tom Chao Zhou, Xin Xin, Junjie Xiong, Yilei Zhang, Yu Kang, Jieming Zhu, and many others. It has been our pleasure to conduct great research work together.

The work described in this paper was fully supported by the National Basic Research Program of China (973 Project No. 2011CB302603), the National Natural Science Foundation of China (Project No. 61100078), the Shenzhen Basic Research Program (Project No. JCYJ20120619153834216, JC201104220300A), and the Research Grants Council of the Hong Kong Special Administrative Region, China (Project No. CUHK 415311).

Contents

Chapter 1
Introduction

Abstract This chapter provides an overview of QoS management of Web services, including background introduction, contributions, and organizations of this book.

Keywords Web service • QoS management

1.1 Overview

Web services are self-contained and self-describing computational Web components designed to support machine-to-machine interaction by programmatic Web method calls [6]. Web services are becoming a major technique for building loosely coupled distributed systems. Examples of service-oriented systems span a variety of diversified application domains, such as e-commerce, automotive systems [1], and multimedia services [5].

As shown in Fig. 1.1, in the service-oriented environment, complex distributed systems are dynamically composed by discovering and integrating distributed Web services, which are provided by different organizations. The distributed Web services are usually employed by more than one service user (i.e., service-oriented systems). The performance of the service-oriented systems is highly reliant on the performance of the employed Web services. Quality of service (QoS) is usually engaged for describing the nonfunctional characteristics of Web services. QoS management of Web services refers to the activities of QoS specification, evaluation, prediction, aggregation, and control of resources to meet end-to-end user and application requirements. With the prevalence of Web services on the Internet, investigating Web service QoS is becoming more and more important.

In recent years, a number of QoS-aware approaches have been comprehensively studied for Web services. However, there is still a lack of real-world Web service QoS datasets for validating new QoS-driven techniques and models. Without convincing and sufficient real-world Web service QoS datasets, characteristics of real-world Web service QoS cannot be fully mined, and the performance of various

Z. Zheng and M.R. Lyu, *QoS Management of Web Services*, Advanced Topics in
Science and Technology in China, DOI 10.1007/978-3-642-34207-3_1,
© Zhejiang University Press, Hangzhou and Springer-Verlag Berlin Heidelberg 2013

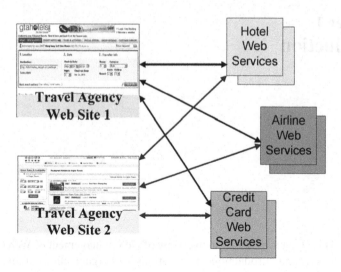

Fig. 1.1 Example of service-oriented system

recently proposed QoS-based approaches cannot be justified. To collect sufficient Web service QoS data, evaluations from different geographic locations under various network conditions are usually required. However, it is not an easy task to conduct large-scale distributed Web service evaluations in reality. An effective and efficient Web service-distributed evaluation mechanism is consequently required.

The Web service evaluation approaches attempt to obtain the Web service QoS values by monitoring the target Web service. However, in some scenarios, a comprehensive Web service evaluation may not be possible (e.g., when the Web service invocation is charged, there are too many service candidates). Therefore, Web service QoS prediction approaches, which require no additional real-world Web service invocations, are becoming more and more attractive. Web service QoS prediction aims at making personalized QoS value prediction for the service users by employing the partially available information (e.g., QoS information of other users, characteristics of the current user, historical QoS performance of the target Web services). To predict the Web service QoS values as accurately as possible, comprehensive investigations of the prediction approaches are needed.

Employing the evaluated/predicted Web service QoS values, QoS-aware fault-tolerant service-oriented systems can be built using redundant Web services on the Internet. Due to the cost of developing redundant components, traditional software fault tolerance [4] is usually employed only for critical systems. In the area of service-oriented computing, however, the cost of developing multiple redundant components is greatly reduced, since the functionally equivalent Web services are provided by different organizations and are accessible via the Internet. These Web services can be employed as alternative components for building fault-tolerant service-oriented systems. Although a number of fault tolerance strategies [2, 3, 7] have been proposed for Web services, the highly dynamic Internet environment requires smarter and more adaptive fault tolerance strategies. Dynamic selection and reconfiguration of the optimal fault tolerance strategy becomes a necessity in service computing.

Based on the above analysis, in order to improve QoS management of Web services, we need to provide efficient Web service QoS evaluation mechanisms, accurate Web service QoS prediction approaches, and robust QoS-aware fault tolerance strategies for Web services. In this book, we propose six approaches to attack these challenging research problems.

The first approach is targeted at Web service evaluation by proposing a distributed Web service QoS evaluation framework. After that, the next three approaches address the Web service QoS prediction problem by employing neighborhood-based, model-based, and ranking-based collaborative filtering techniques. The last two approaches focus on QoS-aware fault tolerance Web services by designing an adaptive fault tolerance strategy and optimal fault tolerance strategy selection framework. The detailed contributions and organizations of these approaches will be presented in Sects. 1.2 and 1.3, respectively.

1.2 Contributions

The main contributions of this book can be described as follows:

- QoS Evaluation of Web Services
  In order to achieve efficient Web service evaluation, we propose a distributed QoS evaluation framework foreb services. This framework employs the concept of user collaboration, which is the key concept of Web 2.0. In our framework, users in different geographic locations share their observed Web service QoS information. The information is stored in a centralized server and will be reused for other users. Several large-scale distributed evaluations are conducted on real-world Web services, and detailed evaluation results are publicly released for future research.[1] Our released Web service QoS datasets have been downloaded by more than 40 research institutes worldwide.

- Neighborhood-Based QoS Prediction of Web Services
  To accurately predict the Web service QoS values, we propose a neighborhood-based collaborative filtering approach for predicting the QoS values for the current user by employing historical Web service QoS data from other similar users. Our approach systematically combines the user-based approach and the item-based approach. Our approach requires no Web service invocations and can help service users discover suitable Web services by analyzing QoS information from their similar users. Moreover, we conducted a large-scale real-world experimental analysis for verifying our QoS prediction result, involving 100

---

[1]http://www.wsdream.net

real-world Web services in 22 countries and 150 service users in 24 countries. The experimental results show that combining the user-based and item-based prediction approaches can achieve more accurate QoS value prediction.

- Model-Based QoS Prediction of Web Services

  The neighborhood-based QoS prediction approach has several drawbacks, including (1) the computation complexity is too high, and (2) it is not easy to find similar users/items when the user-item matrix is very sparse. To address these drawbacks, we propose a neighborhood-integrated matrix factorization (NIMF) approach for Web service QoS value prediction. Our approach explores the social wisdom of service users by systematically fusing the neighborhood-based and the model-based collaborative filtering approaches to achieve higher prediction accuracy. Moreover, we conducted large-scale experiments involving 339 distributed service users and 5,825 real-world Web services. The extensive experimental investigations show that our NIMF approach can achieve higher prediction accuracy than neighborhood-based approaches. The complexity of our method is much better than that of the neighborhood-based prediction approach. Hence, it is scalable to large datasets.

- Ranking-Based QoS Prediction of Web Services

  The neighborhood-based and model-based collaborative filtering approaches usually try to predict the missing values in the user-item matrix as accurately as possible. However, in the ranking-oriented scenarios, accurate missing value prediction may not lead to accurate ranking. To enable accurate Web service QoS ranking, we propose a ranking-based QoS prediction approach. The contributions of this chapter include (1) identifying the critical problem of personalized quality ranking for Web services and proposing a collaborative QoS-driven quality ranking framework to achieve personalized Web service quality ranking; and (2) conducting extensive real-world experiments to study the ranking performance of our proposed algorithm compared with other competing algorithms. The experimental results show the effectiveness of our approach.

- QoS-Aware Fault Tolerance for Web Services

  The highly dynamic Internet environment makes traditional fault tolerance strategies difficult to be used in the service-oriented environment. In this chapter, we propose an adaptive fault tolerance strategy for Web services. The contributions of this chapter are twofold: (1) A QoS-aware middleware for achieving fault tolerance by employing user participation and user collaboration. By encouraging users to contribute their individually obtained QoS information of the target Web services, more accurate evaluation of the Web services can be achieved. (2) An adaptive fault tolerance strategy. We propose an adaptive fault tolerance strategy for automatic system reconfiguration at runtime based on the subject user requirements and objective QoS information of the target Web services.

- QoS-Aware Selection Framework for Web Services

  This chapter aims at advancing the current state of the art in software fault tolerance for Web services by proposing a systematic and extensible framework. The contributions of this chapter are threefold: (1) We propose the first comprehensive fault tolerance strategy selection framework for systematic design, composition, and evaluation of service-oriented systems. Our framework determines optimal fault tolerance strategy dynamically based on the quality-of-service (QoS) performance of Web services as well as the preferences of service users. (2) Different from the previous approaches which mainly focus on stateless Web services, we apply software fault tolerance strategies for the stateful Web services, where multiple tasks have state dependency and must be performed by the same Web services. (3) Large-scale experiments are conducted to verify the proposed selection approach. The experimental results show the effectiveness of our QoS-aware fault tolerance selection framework for Web services.

1.3   Organization

The rest of this book is organized as follows:

- Chapter 2
  In this chapter, we briefly review some background knowledge and related work on QoS management of Web services.
- Chapter 3
  In this chapter, we present a distributed fault tolerance strategy evaluation and selection framework for Web services, which is designed and implemented as WS-DREAM (Distributed Reliability Assessment Mechanism for Web Services) [8, 9, 11]. We first introduce a QoS model of Web service and the system architecture. Then, several large-scale evaluations are conducted on real-world Web services, including six functionally equivalent Amazon Web services and 5,825 publicly available Internet Web services. These evaluations show the effectiveness of our evaluation approach. Reusable Web service QoS datasets are released for future research.
- Chapter 4
  In this chapter, we present a neighborhood-based collaborative filtering approach for providing personalized QoS prediction of Web services [10, 12, 14]. Our approach includes four phases: (1) user similarity computation, (2) similar user selection, (3) missing value prediction of the user-item matrix, and (4) personalized QoS value prediction. In our approach, similar service users are defined as the service users who have similar historical QoS experience on the same set of commonly invoked Web services with the current user. Based on the QoS values from similar users, the missing QoS value for the current user can be accurately predicted. We conducted experiments employing real-world Web service QoS data. The experimental results show the effectiveness of our neighborhood-based QoS prediction approach.

- Chapter 5

  In this chapter, we propose a neighborhood-integrated matrix factorization (NIMF) approach by systematically fusing the neighborhood-based and the model-based collaborative filtering approaches [13]. We first describe the research problem by a toy example. After that, neighborhood similarity computation approaches are presented. By integrating the neighborhood-based prediction approach into the traditional matrix factorization model, we formulate our NIMF prediction approach. Comprehensive complexity analysis of the NIMF approach is provided. Extensive experiments were conducted to study the impact of various parameters and the prediction accuracy. The experimental results show that the NIMF approach achieves better prediction accuracy than other neighborhood-based approaches.

- Chapter 6

  In this chapter, we propose a ranking-based QoS prediction approach for Web services [15]. Our ranking approach is designed as a four-phase process. In phase 1, we calculate the similarity of the users with the current user based on their rankings on the commonly invoked components. Then, in phase 2, a set of similar users are identified. After that, in phase 3, a preference function is defined to present the quality priority of two components. Finally, in phase 4, a greedy order algorithm is proposed to rank the employed components as well as the unemployed components based on the preference function and making use of the past usage experiences of other similar users. The experimental results show that our proposed approach achieves better ranking accuracy than the rating-based collaborative filtering approaches. Comprehensive investigations on the impact of the algorithm parameters are also provided in this chapter.

- Chapter 7

  This chapter presents adaptive fault tolerance strategy for automatic system reconfiguration at runtime based on the user requirements and Web service QoS information. We first introduce a QoS-aware middleware for user Web service QoS information sharing. Then, various fault tolerance strategies as well as user requirements and QoS models are presented. After that, an adaptive fault tolerance strategy is proposed for Web services. A number of experiments are conducted in this chapter. The experimental results show that our QoS-aware adaptive fault tolerance strategy provides better system reliability performance.

- Chapter 8

  This chapter proposes a systematic and extensible framework for QoS-aware fault tolerance strategy selection. The main features of this framework are (1) an extensible QoS model of Web services, (2) various fault tolerance strategies, (3) a QoS composition model of Web services, (4) a consistency-checking algorithm for complex service plans, and (5) various QoS-aware algorithms for optimal fault tolerance strategy determination for both stateless and stateful Web services. Motivating examples and detailed implementations are also presented. The experimental results show that our framework can efficiently determine the most suitable fault tolerance strategies for a service-oriented system at runtime.

- Chapter 9
  The last chapter summarizes this book and provides some future directions that can be further explored.

In order to make each of these chapters self-contained, some critical contents, for example, model definitions or motivations that have appeared in previous chapters, may be briefly reiterated in some chapters.

References

1. Beek MH, Gnesi S, Koch N, Mazzanti F (2008) Formal verification of an automotive scenario in service-oriented computing. In: Proceedings of the 30th international conference on software engineering (ICSE'08). ACM Press, New York, pp 613–622
2. Fang CL, Liang D, Lin F, Lin CC (2007) Fault-tolerant Web services. J Syst Archit 53(1):21–38
3. Luckow A, Schnor B (2008) Service replication in grids: ensuring consistency in a dynamic, failure-prone environment. In: Proceedings of the IEEE international symposium on parallel and distributed processing, Miami, FL, pp 1–7
4. Lyu MR (1995) Software fault tolerance. Trends in software. Wiley, Chichester
5. Scholz A, Buckl C, Kemper A, Knoll A, Heuer J, Winter M (2008) WSAMUSE: Web service architecture for multimedia services. In: Proceedings of the 30th international conference on software engineering (ICSE'08). ACM Press, New York, pp 703–712
6. Zhang LJ, Zhang J, Cai H (2007) Services computing. Springer/Tsinghua University Press, Berlin/Beijing
7. Zhao W (2007) BFT-WS: a Byzantine fault tolerance framework for Web services. In: Proceedings of the 7th international IEEE EDOC conference workshop (EDOCW'07). IEEE Computer Society, Washington, DC, pp 89–96
8. Zheng Z, Lyu MR (2008) A distributed replication strategy evaluation and selection framework for fault-tolerant Web services. In: Proceedings of the 6th international conference on Web services (ICWS'08). IEEE Computer Society, Piscataway, pp 145–152
9. Zheng Z, Lyu MR (2008) WS-DREAM: a distributed reliability assessment mechanism for Web services. In: Proceedings of the 38th international conference on dependable systems and networks (DSN'08), Anchorage, Alaska, USA, pp 392–397
10. Zheng Z, Lyu MR (2010) Collaborative reliability prediction for service-oriented systems. In: Proceedings of the IEEE/ACM 32nd international conference on software engineering (ICSE'10), Cape Town, South Africa, pp 35–44
11. Zheng Z, Lyu MR (2010) Optimal fault tolerance strategy selection for Web services. Int J Web Serv Res (JWSR) 7(4):21–40
12. Zheng Z, Ma H, Lyu MR, King I (2009) WSRec: a collaborative filtering based Web service recommender system. In: Proceedings of the 7th international conference on Web services (ICWS'09), Los Angeles, CA, USA, pp 437–444
13. Zheng Z, Ma H, Lyu MR, King I (2011) Collaborative Web service QoS prediction via neighborhood integrated matrix factorization. IEEE Trans Serv Comput, accepted
14. Zheng Z, Ma H, Lyu MR, King I (2011) QoS-aware Web service recommendation by collaborative filtering. IEEE Trans Serv Comput 4(2):140–152
15. Zheng Z, Zhang Y, Lyu MR (2010) CloudRank: a QoS-driven component ranking framework for cloud computing. In: Proceedings of the international symposium on reliable distributed systems (SRDS'10), New Delhi, India, pp 184–193

Chapter 2
Background Review

Abstract This chapter reviews related work, including QoS evaluation of Web services, QoS prediction of Web services, and fault-tolerant Web services.

Keywords QoS evaluation • QoS prediction • Fault-tolerant

2.1 QoS Evaluation of Web Services

In the field of service computing [77], Web services QoS have been discussed in a number of research investigations for presenting the nonfunctional characteristics of the Web services [30, 47, 49, 50, 55, 67]. Zeng et al. [76] employ five generic QoS properties (i.e., execution price, execution duration, reliability, availability, and reputation) for dynamic Web service composition. Ardagna et al. [3] use five QoS properties (i.e., execution time, availability, price, reputation, and data quality) when making adaptive service composition in flexible processes. Alrifai et al. [2] propose an efficient service composition approach by considering both generic QoS properties and domain-specific QoS properties.

QoS measurement of Web services has been used in the service level agreement (SLA) [43], such as IBM's WSLA framework [33] and the work from HP [56]. In SLA, the QoS data are mainly for the service providers to maintain a certain level of service to their clients, and the QoS data are not available to others. In this book, we mainly focus on encouraging the service users to share their individually obtained QoS data of the Web services, making efficient and effective Web service evaluation and selection.

Based on the QoS performance of Web services, various approaches have been proposed for Web service selection [5, 6, 11, 26, 75, 79], Web service composition [2, 3, 10, 11, 76], fault-tolerant Web services [20, 42, 78, 80, 82, 83, 91], Web service recommendation [15, 86, 88], Web service reliability prediction [12, 17, 22, 24, 25, 72, 84], Web service search [90], and so on. Various QoS-aware approaches, such as QoS-aware middleware [76], adaptive service composition [3], efficient service

Z. Zheng and M.R. Lyu, *QoS Management of Web Services*, Advanced Topics in Science and Technology in China, DOI 10.1007/978-3-642-34207-3_2,
© Zhejiang University Press, Hangzhou and Springer-Verlag Berlin Heidelberg 2013

selection algorithms [75], reputation conceptual model [46], and Bayesian network-based assessment model [70], have been proposed recently. Some recent work also takes subjective information (e.g., provider reputations, user requirements) into consideration to enable more accurate Web service selection [18, 55]. Although various QoS-aware approaches have been comprehensively studied for Web services, there is a lack of a real-world Web service QoS dataset for verifying these approaches. To obtain the Web service QoS values for a certain user, distributed Web service evaluations from the client side are usually required [18, 46, 70].

Web service evaluation is a task to evaluate the discovered Web services with respect to user requests. Real-world Web service evaluations from distributed locations are not an easy task. In our previous work [79, 81, 85], a real-world Web service evaluation has been conducted by 5 service users on 8 publicly accessible Web services. Since the scale of this experiment is too small, the experimental results are not scalable for future research. Al-Masri et al. [1] released a Web service QoS dataset which was observed by only 1 service user on 2,507 Web services. The fact that different users will observe quite different QoS of the same Web service limits the applicability of this dataset. Our recently released datasets [90], on the other hand, include QoS information observed from distributed service users. Moreover, the scales of our datasets are much larger ($339 \times 5,825$). Vieira et al. [68] conducted an experimental evaluation of security vulnerabilities in 300 publicly available Web services. Security vulnerabilities usually exist at the server side and are user-independent (different users observe the same security vulnerabilities on the target Web service). Different from Vieira's work [68], this book mainly focuses on investigating performance of user-dependent QoS properties (e.g., failure probabilities, response time, and throughput), which can vary widely among different users.

2.2 QoS Prediction of Web Services

Collaborative filtering methods are widely adopted in recommender systems [8, 44, 54]. Three types of collaborative filtering approaches are widely studied: neighborhood-based (memory-based), model-based, and ranking-based.

The most analyzed examples of memory-based collaborative filtering include user-based approaches [7, 27, 31], item-based approaches [19, 39, 62], and their fusion [69, 86]. User-based approaches predict the ratings of active users based on the ratings of their similar users, and item-based approaches predict the ratings of active users based on the computed information of items similar to those chosen by the active users. User-based and item-based approaches often use the PCC algorithm [54] and the VSS algorithm [7] as the similarity computation methods. PCC-based collaborative filtering generally can achieve higher performance than VSS, since it considers the differences in the user rating style. Wang et al. [69] combined user-based and item-based collaborative filtering approaches for movie recommendation.

In the model-based collaborative filtering approaches, training datasets are used to train a predefined model. Examples of model-based approaches include the

clustering model [71], aspect models [28, 29, 65], and the latent factor model [9].
Kohrs and Merialdo [35] present an algorithm for collaborative filtering based on
hierarchical clustering, which tries to balance robustness and accuracy of predictions, especially when few data are available. Hofmann [28] proposes an algorithm
based on a generalization of probabilistic latent semantic analysis to continuous-
valued response variables. Recently, several matrix factorization methods [45, 53,
57, 58] have been proposed for collaborative filtering. These methods focus on
fitting the user-item matrix with low-rank approximations, which is engaged to
make further predictions. The premise behind a low-dimensional factor model is
that there are only a small number of factors influencing the values in the user-item
matrix and that a user's factor vector is determined by how each factor applies to that
user. The neighborhood-based methods utilize the values of similar users or items
(local information) for making value prediction, while model-based methods, like
matrix factorization models, employ all the value information of the matrix (global
information) for making value prediction.

The neighborhood-based and model-based collaborative filtering approaches
usually try to predict the missing values in the user-item matrix as accurately as
possible. However, in the ranking-oriented scenarios, accurate missing value prediction may not lead to accuracy ranking. Therefore, ranking-oriented collaborative
filtering approaches are becoming more and more attractive. Liu et al. [40] propose
a ranking-oriented collaborative filtering approach to rank movies. Yang et al. [73]
propose another ranking-oriented approach for ranking books in digital libraries.

There is limited work in the literature employing collaborative filtering methods
for Web service QoS value prediction. One of the most important reasons that
obstruct the research is that there is no large-scale real-world Web service QoS
dataset available for studying the prediction accuracy. Without convincing and
sufficient real-world Web service QoS data, the characteristics of Web service
QoS information cannot be fully mined, and the performance of the proposed
algorithms cannot be justified. A few approaches [32, 66] mention the idea of
applying neighborhood-based collaborative filtering methods for Web service QoS
value prediction. However, these approaches simply employ a movie-rating dataset,
that is, MovieLens [54], for experimental studies, which is not convincing enough.
Shao et al. [63] propose a user-based PCC method for the Web service QoS value
prediction. However, only 20 Web services are involved in the experiments. In this
book, we propose various approaches to address the problem of Web service QoS
prediction, including neighborhood-based [86, 88], model-based [87], and ranking-
based approaches [89].

2.3 Fault-Tolerant Web Services

Software fault tolerance is widely employed for building reliable stand-alone
systems as well as distributed systems [23]. The major software fault tolerance
techniques include recovery block [52], N-Version Programming (NVP) [4], N self-
checking programming [37], distributed recovery block [34], and so on.

In the area of service-oriented computing, the cost of developing redundant components is greatly reduced, since the functionally equivalent Web services can be employed for building diversity-based fault-tolerant service-oriented systems [20, 41]. A number of service fault tolerance strategies have been proposed in the recent literature [13, 14, 21, 60, 82]. The major fault tolerance strategies for Web services can be divided into passive strategies and active strategies. Passive strategies have been discussed in FT-SOAP [20], FT-CORBA [64], and in work [16]. Active strategies have been investigated in FTWeb [61], Thema [48], WS-Replication [59], SWS [38], and Perpetual [51].

Work [60] employs a rigorous development process to build a reliable connector, which is a critical component. The connector is implemented as a Web service using the original WSDL description of the Web service replicas. Within the connector, lots of fault tolerance strategies can be implemented (e.g., active or passive replication strategies). FTWeb [61] proposes a WSDispatcher to make parallel Web service invocations and to return the final result to the users. Work [38] proposes a survivable Web service framework named SWS. In SWS, each Web service is replicated and deployed onto a set of nodes to form a Web service group. All the replicas are invoked to process the same user request independently. Value faults can thus be tolerated by majority voting. Moreover, SWS supports continuous operation in the presence of Byzantine faults [36]. Ye et al. [74] propose a middleware, PWSS, to support a client transparent active replication strategy. When a client sends a request r, r is first sent to a PWSS. This PWSS then multicasts r to all other PWSSs. After agreeing a total order on threads execution, all the replicas process the client's request and return the response to a PWSS which first received the client. This PWSS then returns a result to the client's invocation after running a voting strategy on all the responses it received. Thema [48] is a Byzantine fault-tolerant (BFT) middleware for Web services which supports three-tiered application model. $3f + 1$ Web service replicas in the server side need to invoke an external Web service for accomplishing their executions.

Different from the previous work, in this book, we will present an adaptive fault tolerance strategy for Web services [80, 83] and propose a QoS-aware selection framework for fault-tolerant Web services [82].

References

1. Al-Masri E, Mahmoud QH (2008) Investigating Web services on the World Wide Web. In: Proceedings of the 17th international conference on World Wide Web (WWW'08), Beijing, China, pp 795–804
2. Alrifai M, Risse T (2009) Combining global optimization with local selection for efficient QoS-aware service composition. In: Proceedings of the 18th international conference on World Wide Web (WWW'09), Madrid, Spain, pp 881–890
3. Ardagna D, Pernici B (2007) Adaptive service composition in flexible processes. IEEE Trans Softw Eng 33(6):369–384

4. Avizienis A (1995) The methodology of N-version programming. In: Lyu MR (ed) Software fault tolerance. Wiley, Chichester, pp 23–46
5. Bilgin AS, Singh MP (2004) A DAML-based repository for QoS-aware semantic Web service selection. In: Proceedings of the 2nd international conference on Web services (ICWS'04), San Diego, CA, pp 368–375
6. Bonatti PA, Festa P (2005) On optimal service selection. In: Proceedings of the 14th international conference on World Wide Web (WWW'05), Chiba, Japan, pp 530–538
7. Breese JS, Heckerman D, Kadie C (1998) Empirical analysis of predictive algorithms for collaborative filtering. In: Proceedings of the 14th annual conference on uncertainty in artificial intelligence (UAI'98), San Francisco, CA, pp 43–52
8. Burke R (2002) Hybrid recommender systems: survey and experiments. User Model User Adapt Interact 12(4):331–370
9. Canny J (2002) Collaborative filtering with privacy via factor analysis. In: Proceedings of the 25th international ACM SIGIR conference on research and development in information retrieval (SIGIR'02), Tampere, Finland, pp 238–245
10. Cardellini V, Casalicchio E, Grassi V, Lo Presti F, Mirandola R (2009) QoS-driven runtime adaptation of service oriented architectures. In: Proceedings of the 7th joint meeting European software engineering conference and ACM SIGSOFT symposium on foundations of s engineering (ESEC/FSE'09), Amsterdam, The Netherlands, pp 131–140
11. Cardellini V, Casalicchio E, Grassi V, Presti FL (2007) Flow-based service selection for Web service composition supporting multiple QoS classes. In: Proceedings of the 5th international conference on Web services (ICWS'07), Salt Lake City, UT, pp 743–750
12. Cardoso J, Miller J, Sheth A, Arnold J (2002) Modeling quality of service for workflows and Web service processes. J Web Semant 1:281–308
13. Chan PPW, Lyu MR, Malek M (2006) Making services fault tolerant. In: Proceedings of the 3rd international service availability symposium (ISAS'06), Helsinki, Finland, pp 43–61
14. Chan PP, Lyu MR, Malek M (2007) Reliable Web services: methodology, experiment and modeling. In: Proceedings of the 5th international conference on Web services (ICWS'07), Salt Lake City, UT, pp 679–686
15. Chen X, Lyu MR (2003) Message logging and recovery in wireless corba using access bridge. In: The 6th international symposium on autonomous decentralized systems, Pisa, Italy, pp 107–114
16. Chen X, Liu X, Huang Z, Sun H (2010) RegionKNN: a scalable hybrid collaborative filtering algorithm for personalized Web service recommendation. In: Proceedings of the 8th international conference on Web services (ICWS'10), Miami, FL, pp 9–16
17. Cheung RC (1980) A user-oriented software reliability model. IEEE Trans Softw Eng 6(2):118–125
18. Deora V, Shao J, Gray W, Fiddian N (2003) A quality of service management framework based on user expectations. In: Proceedings of the 1st international conference on service-oriented computing (ICSOC'03), Trento, Italy, pp 104–114
19. Deshpande M, Karypis G (2004) Item-based top-n recommendation. ACM Trans Inf Syst 22(1):143–177
20. Fang CL, Liang D, Lin F, Lin CC (2007) Fault-tolerant Web services. J Syst Architect 53(1):21–38
21. Foster H, Uchitel S, Magee J, Kramer J (2003) Model-based verification of Web service compositions. In: Proceedings of the 18th IEEE international conference on automated software engineering (ASE'03), Montreal, Quebec, Canada, pp 152–161
22. Gokhale SS, Trivedi KS (2002) Reliability prediction and sensitivity analysis based on software architecture. In: Proceedings of the international symposium on software reliability engineering (ISSRE'02), Annapolis, MD, pp 64–78
23. Gorender S, de Araujo Macedo RJ, Raynal M (2007) An adaptive programming model for fault-tolerant distributed computing. IEEE Trans Depend Secure Comput 4(1):18–31
24. Goseva-Popstojanova K, Trivedi KS (2001) Architecture-based approach to reliability assessment of software systems. Perform Eval 45(2–3):179–204

25. Grassi V, Patella S (2006) Reliability prediction for service-oriented computing environments. IEEE Internet Comput 10(3):43–49
26. Haddad JE, Manouvrier M, Ramirez G, RukozM (2008) QoS-driven selection of Web services for transactional composition. In: Proceedings of the 6th international conference on Web services (ICWS'08), Beijing, China, pp 653–660
27. Herlocker JL, Konstan JA, Borchers A, Riedl J (1999) An algorithmic framework for performing collaborative filtering. In: Proceedings of the 22nd international ACM SIGIR conference on research and development in information retrieval (SIGIR'99), Berkeley, CA, pp 230–237
28. Hofmann T (2003) Collaborative filtering via Gaussian probabilistic latent semantic analysis. In: Proceedings of the 26th international ACM SIGIR conference on research and development in information retrieval (SIGIR'03), Toronto, Canada, pp 259–266
29. Hofmann T (2004) Latent semantic models for collaborative filtering. ACM Trans Inf Syst 22(1):89–115
30. Jaeger MC, Rojec-Goldmann G, Muhl G (2004) QoS aggregation for Web service composition using workflow patterns. In: Proceedings of the 8th IEEE international conference on enterprise computing, Monterey, CA, pp 149–159
31. Jin R, Chai JY, Si L (2004) An automatic weighting scheme for collaborative filtering. In: Proceedings of the 27th international ACM SIGIR conference on research and development in information retrieval (SIGIR'04), Sheffield, UK, pp 337–344
32. Karta K (2005) An investigation on personalized collaborative filtering for Web service selection. Honours Programme thesis, University of Western Australia, Brisbane
33. Keller A, Ludwig H (2002) The WSLA framework: specifying and monitoring service level agreements for Web services. IBM Research Division
34. Kim K, Welch H (1989) Distributed execution of recovery blocks: an approach for uniform treatment of hardware and software faults in real-time applications. IEEE Trans Comput 38(5):626–636
35. Kohrs A, Merialdo B (1999) Clustering for collaborative filtering applications. In: Proceedings of the international conference on computational intelligence for modelling, control and automation. Ios Press, Amsterdam, pp 199–204
36. Lamport L, Shostak R, Pease M (1982) The Byzantine generals problem. ACM Trans Program Lang Syst 4(3):382–401
37. Laprie J, Arlat J, Beounes C, Kanoun K (1990) Definition and analysis of hardware and software fault-tolerant architectures. Computer 23(7):39–51
38. Li W, He J, Ma Q, Yen IL, Bastani F, Paul R (2005) A framework to support survivable Web services. In: Proceedings of the 19th IEEE international symposium on parallel and distributed processing, Denver, Colorado, USA, pp 93–94
39. Linden G, Smith B, York J (2003) Amazon.com recommendations: item-to-item collaborative filtering. IEEE Internet Comput 7(1):76–80
40. Liu NN, Yang Q (2008) Eigenrank: a ranking-oriented approach to collaborative filtering. In: Proceedings of the 31st international ACM SIGIR conference on research and development in information retrieval (SIGIR'08), Singapore, pp 83–90
41. Looker N, Munro M, Xu J (2005) Increasing Web service dependability through consensus voting. In: Proceedings of the 29th international computer software and applications conference, Edinburgh, Scotland, UK, vol 2, pp 66–69
42. Luckow A, Schnor B (2008) Service replication in grids: ensuring consistency in a dynamic, failure-prone environment. In: Proceedings of the IEEE international symposium on parallel and distributed processing, Miami, FL, pp 1–7
43. Ludwig H, Keller A, Dan A, King R, Franck R (2003) A service level agreement language for dynamic electronic services. Electron Commer Res 3(1–2):43–59
44. Ma H, King I, Lyu MR (2007) Effective missing data prediction for collaborative filtering. In: Proceedings of the 30th international ACM SIGIR conference on research and development in information retrieval (SIGIR'07), Amsterdam, The Netherlands, pp 39–46

45. Ma H, King I, Lyu MR (2009) Learning to recommend with social trust ensemble. In: Proceedings of the 32nd international ACM SIGIR conference on research and development in information retrieval (SIGIR'09), Boston, MA, USA, pp 203–210
46. Maximilien E, Singh M (2002) Conceptual model of Web service reputation. ACM SIGMOD Rec 31(4):36–41
47. Menasce DA (2002) QoS issues in Web services. IEEE Internet Comput 6(6):72–75
48. Merideth MG, Iyengar A, Mikalsen T, Tai S, Rouvellou I, Narasimhan P (2005) Thema: Byzantine fault-tolerant middleware for Web service applications. In: Proceedings of the 24th IEEE symposium on reliable distributed systems (SRDS'05), Orlando, FL, pp 131–142
49. O'Sullivan J, Edmond D, ter Hofstede AHM (2002) What's in a service? Distrib Parallel Databases 12(2/3):117–133
50. Ouzzani M, Bouguettaya A (2004) Efficient access to Web services. IEEE Internet Comput 8(2):34–44
51. Pallemulle SL, Thorvaldsson HD, Goldman KJ (2008) Byzantine fault-tolerant Web services for n-tier and service oriented architectures. In: Proceedings of the 28th international conference on distributed computing systems (ICDCS'08), Beijing, China, pp 260–268
52. Randell B, Xu J (1995) The evolution of the recovery block concept. In: Lyu MR (ed) Software fault tolerance. Wiley, Chichester, pp 1–21
53. Rennie JDM, Srebro N (2005) Fast maximum margin matrix factorization for collaborative prediction. In: Proceedings of the 22nd international conference on machine learning (ICML'05), Bonn, Germany, pp 713–719
54. Resnick P, Iacovou N, Suchak M, Bergstrom P, Riedl J (1994) Grouplens: an open architecture for collaborative filtering of netnews. In: Proceedings of the ACM conference on computer supported cooperative work, Chapel Hill, North Carolina, USA, pp 175–186
55. Rosario S, Benveniste A, Haar S, Jard C (2008) Probabilistic QoS and soft contracts for transaction-based Web services orchestrations. IEEE Trans Serv Comput 1(4):187–200
56. Sahai A, Durante A, Machiraju V (2002) Towards automated SLA management for Web services. HP Laboratory
57. Salakhutdinov R, Mnih A (2007) Probabilistic matrix factorization. In: Proceedings of the advances in neural information processing systems, Vancouver, British Columbia, Canada, pp 1257–1264
58. Salakhutdinov R, Mnih A (2008) Bayesian probabilistic matrix factorization using markov chain Monte Carlo. In: Proceedings of the 25th international conference on machine learning (ICML'08), Helsinki, Finland, pp 880–887
59. Salas J, Perez-Sorrosal F, Marta Pati NM, Jiménez-Peris R (2006) WSReplication: a framework for highly available Web services. In: Proceedings of the 15th international conference on World Wide Web (WWW'06), Edinburgh, Scotland, pp 357–366
60. Salatge N, Fabre JC (2007) Fault tolerance connectors for unreliable Web services. In: Proceedings of the 37th international conference on dependable systems and networks (DSN'07), Edinburgh, UK, pp 51–60
61. Santos GT, Lung LC, Montez C (2005) FTWeb: a fault tolerant infrastructure for Web services. In: Proceedings of the 9th IEEE international conference on enterprise computing, Enschede, the Netherlands, pp 95–105
62. Sarwar B, Karypis G, Konstan J, Riedl J (2001) Item-based collaborative filtering recommendation algorithms. In: Proceedings of the 10th international conference on World Wide Web (WWW'01), Hong Kong, China, pp 285–295
63. Shao L, Zhang J, Wei Y, Zhao J, Xie B, Mei H (2007) Personalized QoS prediction for Web services via collaborative filtering. In: Proceedings of the 5th international conference on Web services (ICWS'07), Salt Lake City, UT, pp 439–446
64. Sheu GW, Chang YS, Liang D, Yuan SM, LoW (1997) A fault-tolerant object service on CORBA. In: Proceedings of the 17th international conference on distributed computing systems (ICDCS'97), Baltimore, Maryland, USA, pp 393
65. Si L, Jin R (2003) Flexible mixture model for collaborative filtering. In: Proceedings of the 20th international conference on machine learning (ICML'03), Washington, DC, USA, pp 704–711

66. Sreenath RM, Singh MP (2003) Agent-based service selection. J Web Semant 1(3):261–279
67. Thio N, Karunasekera S (2005) Automatic measurement of a QoS metric for Web service recommendation. In: Proceedings of the Australian software engineering conference, pp 202–211
68. Vieira M, Antunes N, Madeira H (2009) Using Web security scanners to detect vulnerabilities in Web services. In: Proceedings of the 39th international conference on dependable systems and networks (DSN'09), Estoril, Lisbon, Portugal, pp 566–571
69. Wang J, de Vries AP, Reinders MJ (2006) Unifying user-based and item-based collaborative filtering approaches by similarity fusion. In: Proceedings of the 29th international ACM SIGIR conference on research and development in information retrieval (SIGIR'06), Seattle, Washington, USA, pp 501–508
70. Wu G, Wei J, Qiao X, Li L (2007) A Bayesian network based QoS assessment model for Web services. In: Proceedings of the international conference on services computing (SCC'07), Salt Lake City, UT, pp 498–505
71. Xue G, Lin C, Yang Q, Xi W, Zeng H, Yu Y, Chen Z (2005) Scalable collaborative filtering using cluster-based smoothing. In: Proceedings of the 28th international ACM SIGIR conference on research and development in information retrieval (SIGIR'05), Salvador, Brazil, pp 114–121
72. Yacoub SM, Cukic B, Ammar HH (1999) Scenario-based reliability analysis of component-based software. In: Proceedings of the international symposium on software reliability engineering (ISSRE'99), Boca Raton, FL, pp 22–31
73. Yang C, Wei B, Wu J, Zhang Y, Zhang L (2009) CARES: a ranking-oriented cadal recommender system. In: Proceedings of the 9th ACM/IEEE-CS joint conference on digital libraries (JCDL'09), Austin, TX, USA, pp 203–212
74. Ye X, Shen Y (2005) Replicating multithreaded Web services. In: Proceedings of the 3rd international symposium on parallel and distributed processing and applications, Nanjing, China
75. Yu T, Zhang Y, Lin KJ (2007) Efficient algorithms for Web services selection with end-to-end QoS constraints. ACM Trans Web 1(1):1–26
76. Zeng L, Benatallah B, Ngu AH, Dumas M, Kalagnanam J, Chang H (2004) QoS-aware middleware for Web services composition. IEEE Trans Softw Eng 30(5):311–327
77. Zhang LJ, Zhang J, Cai H (2007) Services computing. Springer/Tsinghua University Press, Berlin/Beijing
78. Zhao W (2007) BFT-WS: a Byzantine fault tolerance framework for Web services. In: Proceedings of the 7th international IEEE EDOC conference on workshop (EDOCW'07), Annapolis, MD, pp 89–96
79. Zheng Z, Lyu MR (2008) A distributed replication strategy evaluation and selection framework for fault-tolerant Web services. In: Proceedings of the 6th international conference on Web services (ICWS'08), Beijing, China, pp 145–152
80. Zheng Z, Lyu MR (2008) A QoS-aware middleware for fault tolerant Web services. In: Proceedings of the international symposium on software reliability engineering (ISSRE'08), Seattle, USA, pp 97–106
81. Zheng Z, Lyu MR (2008) WS-DREAM: a distributed reliability assessment mechanism for Web services. In: Proceedings of the 38th international conference on dependable systems and networks (DSN'08), Anchorage, Alaska, USA, pp 392–397
82. Zheng Z, Lyu MR (2009) A QoS-aware fault tolerant middleware for dependable service composition. In: Proceedings of the 39th International conference on dependable systems and networks (DSN'09), Lisbon, Portugal, pp 239–248
83. Zheng Z, Lyu MR (2010) An adaptive QoS-aware fault tolerance strategy for Web services. Springer J Empir Softw Eng (EMSE) 15(5):323–345
84. Zheng Z, Lyu MR (2010) Collaborative reliability prediction for service-oriented systems. In: Proceedings of the IEEE/ACM 32nd international conference on software engineering (ICSE'10), Cape Town, South Africa, pp 35–44

85. Zheng Z, Lyu MR (2010) Optimal fault tolerance strategy selection for Web services. Int J Web Serv Res (JWSR) 7(4):21–40
86. Zheng Z, Ma H, Lyu MR, King I (2009) WSRec: a collaborative filtering based Web service recommender system. In: Proceedings of the 7th international conference on Web services (ICWS'09), Los Angeles, CA, pp 437–444
87. Zheng Z, Ma H, Lyu MR, King I (2011) Collaborative Web service QoS prediction via neighborhood integrated matrix factorization. IEEE Trans Serv Comput, accepted
88. Zheng Z, Ma H, Lyu MR, King I (2011) QoS-aware Web service recommendation by collaborative filtering. IEEE Trans Serv Comput 4(2):140–152
89. Zheng Z, Zhang Y, Lyu MR (2010) CloudRank: a QoS-driven component ranking framework for cloud computing. In: Proceedings of the international symposium on reliable distributed systems (SRDS'10), New Delhi, India, pp 184–193
90. Zheng Z, Zhang Y, Lyu MR (2010) Distributed QoS evaluation for real-world Web services. In: Proceedings of the 8th international conference on Web services (ICWS'10), Miami, FL, pp 83–90
91. Zheng Z, Zhou TC, Lyu MR, King I (2010) FTCloud: a ranking-based framework for fault tolerant cloud applications. In: Proceedings of the international symposium on software reliability engineering (ISSRE'10), CA, US, pp 398–407

Chapter 3
QoS Evaluation of Web Services

Abstract In order to achieve efficient Web service evaluation, this chapter proposes a distributed QoS evaluation framework for Web services. The proposed framework employs the concept of user collaboration, which is the key concept of Web 2.0. In our framework, users in different geographic locations share their observed Web service QoS information. The information is stored in a centralized server and will be reused for other users. Several large-scale distributed evaluations are conducted on real-world Web services, and detailed evaluation results are publicly released for future research.

Keywords Service evaluation · User collaboration · Distributed evaluation

3.1 Overview

Web services have been emerging in recent years and are by now one of the most popular techniques for building versatile distributed systems. The performance of the service-oriented systems is highly reliant on the performance of the employed Internet Web services. With the prevalence of Web services on the Internet, investigating the quality of Web services is becoming more and more important.

Quality of service (QoS), which is usually employed for describing the non-functional characteristics of Web services, has become an important differentiating point of different Web services [10]. Different Web service QoS properties can be divided into user-independent QoS properties and user-dependent QoS properties. Values of the user-independent QoS properties (e.g., price, popularity) are usually advertised by service providers and identical for different users. On the other hand, values of the user-dependent QoS properties (e.g., failure probability, response time, throughput) can vary widely for different users influenced by the unpredictable Internet connections and the heterogeneous user environments.

In the field of service computing [15], a lot of QoS-driven approaches have been proposed for Web service selection [3, 5, 8, 13], optimal service composition

Z. Zheng and M.R. Lyu, *QoS Management of Web Services*, Advanced Topics in
Science and Technology in China, DOI 10.1007/978-3-642-34207-3_3,
© Zhejiang University Press, Hangzhou and Springer-Verlag Berlin Heidelberg 2013

[1, 2, 5, 14], fault-tolerant Web services [7, 18], Web service recommendation [20], Web service reliability prediction [19], and so on. However, there is still a lack of real-world Web service QoS datasets for validating new QoS-driven techniques and models. To provide comprehensive studies of the user-independent QoS properties of real-world Web services, evaluations from different geographic locations under various network conditions are usually required. However, it is difficult to conduct large-scale Web service evaluations from distributed locations, since Web service invocations consume resources of the service providers and impose costs for the service users. Moreover, it is difficult to collect Web service QoS data from the distributed service users.

To attack this critical challenge, we propose a distributed evaluation framework for Web services and conducted several large-scale distributed evaluations on real-world Web services. The evaluation results (e.g., Web service addresses, WSDL files, all the evaluation results) were publicly released for future research.[1] The released datasets can be employed by a lot of QoS-aware research topics on Web services.

The rest of this chapter is organized as follows: Sect. 3.2 introduces our distributed Web service QoS evaluation framework. Section 3.3 presents our primary evaluation results on the Amazon Web services. Section 3.4 shows our large-scale evaluation of the publicly available Web services, and Sect. 3.5 concludes this chapter.

3.2 Distributed QoS Evaluation Framework

3.2.1 QoS Model of Web Services

In the presence of multiple service candidates with identical or similar functionalities, quality of service (QoS) provides nonfunctional characteristics for the optimal candidate selection. Based on the previous investigations [2, 10, 14], we identify the most representative QoS properties of Web services in the following:

- Availability (av) q^1: the percentage of time that a Web service is operating during a certain time interval.
- Price (pr) q^2: the fee that a service user has to pay for invoking a Web service.
- Popularity (po) q^3: the number of received invocations of a Web service during a certain time interval.
- Data size (ds) q^4: the size of the Web service invocation response.
- Failure probability (fp) q^5: the probability that a request has failed. In this book, failure probability and failure rate are interchangeable.

---

[1]http://www.wsdream.net

- Response time (rt) q^6: the time duration between a service user sending a request and receiving a response. In this book, response time and RTT (round-trip time) are interchangeable.

In the above QoS model, q^1 to q^4 are user-independent QoS properties, which are provided by the service providers and are the same for all the service users. q^5 and q^6 are user-dependent QoS properties, which should be measured at the client side since they are affected by the communication links. This QoS model is extensible, where more quality properties can be added in the future without fundamental changes. Given the above QoS properties, the QoS performance of a Web service can be presented as $q = (q^1, \ldots, q^6)$.

3.2.2 System Architecture

Since the service providers may not deliver the QoS they declared and some QoS properties (e.g., response time and failure probability) are highly related to the locations and network conditions of service users, Web service evaluation can be performed at the client side to obtain more accurate QoS performance [12, 14]. However, several challenges have to be solved when conducting Web service evaluation at the client side: (1) It is difficult for the service users to make professional evaluation of the Web services themselves, since the service users are usually not experts of Web service evaluation, which includes WSDL file analysis, test case generation, evaluation mechanism implementation, test result interpretation, and so on; (2) it is time consuming and resource consuming for the service users to conduct a long-duration evaluation of many Web service candidates themselves; and (3) the common time-to-market constraints limit an in-depth and accurate evaluation of the target Web services.

To address these challenges, we propose a distributed evaluation framework for Web services, together with its prototyping system WS-DREAM [16, 17], as shown in Fig. 3.1. This framework employs the concept of user collaboration, which has contributed to the recent success of BitTorrent [4] and Wikipedia.[2] In this framework, users in different geographic locations share their observed QoS performance of Web services by contributing them to a centralized server. Historical evaluation results saved in a data center are available for other service users. In this way, QoS performance of Web services becomes easy to obtain for the service users.

As shown in Fig. 3.1, the proposed distributed evaluation framework includes a centralized server with a number of distributed clients. The overall procedures can be explained as follows:

1. Registration: Service users submit evaluation requests with related information, such as the target Web service addresses, to the WS-DREAM server.

---

[2]http://www.wikipedia.org

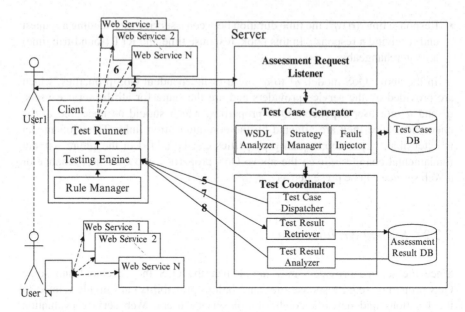

Fig. 3.1 Distributed evaluation framework

2. Client-side application loading: A client-side evaluation application is loaded to the service user's computer.
3. Test case generation: The *Test Case Generator* in the server automatically creates test cases based on the interface of the target Web services (WSDL files).
4. Test coordination: Test tasks are scheduled based on the number of current users and test cases.
5. Test cases retrieval: The distributed client-side evaluation applications get test cases from the centralized server.
6. Test cases execution: The distributed client-side applications execute the test cases to conduct testing on the target Web services.
7. Test result collection: The distributed client-side applications send back the test results to the server and repeat the steps 5, 6, and 7 to retrieve and execute more test cases.
8. Test result analysis: The *Test Result Analyzer* in the server side is engaged to process the collected data and send back the detailed evaluation results to the service user.

The advantages of this user-collaborated evaluation framework include:

1. This framework can be implemented and launched by a trustworthy third party to help service users conduct accurate and efficient Web service evaluation in an easy way, without requiring service users to have professional knowledge of evaluation design, test case generation, test result interpretation, and so on.

Table 3.1 The redundant
Web service candidates

WS group	WSID	Provider	Location
E-commerce service	a1	Amazon	USA
	a2	Amazon	Japan
	a3	Amazon	Germany
	a4	Amazon	Canada
	a5	Amazon	France
	a6	Amazon	UK

2. The historical evaluation results on the same Web services can be reused, making the evaluation more efficient and save resources for both the service users and service providers.
3. The overall evaluation results from different service users can be used as useful information for optimal Web service selection. The assumption is that the Web service, which has good historical performance observed by most of the service users, has a higher probability of providing good service to the new service users.

By this framework, evaluation of Web services becomes accurate, efficient, and effective. Employing this distributed Web service QoS evaluation framework, we conducted several large-scale evaluations of real-world Web services, including the Amazon Web services and a lot of other publicly available Internet Web services. The evaluation results will be introduction in Sects. 3.3 and 3.4.

3.3   Evaluation 1: Amazon Web Services

This section presents our distributed evaluation results of six Amazon Web services.[3] As shown in Table 3.1, these functionally equivalent Web services are deployed in different locations by Amazon.

Table 3.2 and Fig. 3.2 show the experiment results from the six distributed service users (us, hk, sg, cn, tw, and au) on the Amazon Web services (a1–a6). In Table 3.2, under the location column, U stands for user locations, and WS presents the Web services. cn, tw, au, sg, hk, and us present the six user locations conducting the evaluation. As shown in Table 3.1, a1, a2, a3, a4, a5, and a6 stand for the six Amazon Web services, which are located in the USA, Japan, Germany, Canada, France, and the UK, respectively. The cases column shows the failure probability (F%), which is the number of failed invocations (Fail) divided by the number of all invocations (All). The RTT column shows the average (Avg) and standard deviation (SD) of the response-time/round-trip-time (RTT) performance. The ProT column shows the average (Avg) and standard deviation (SD) of the process time (ProT), which is the time consumed by the Web service server for processing the request

---

[3]http://aws.amazon.com/associates

Table 3.2 Evaluation Results of the Amazon Web Services

Location		Cases			RTT (ms)		ProT (ms)	
U	WS	All	Fail	F%	Avg	SD	Avg	SD
cn	a1	484	109	22.52	4,184	2,348	42	19
	a2	482	128	26.55	3,892	2,515	46	27
	a3	487	114	23.40	3,666	2,604	42	17
	a4	458	111	24.23	4,074	2,539	45	21
	a5	498	96	19.27	3,654	2,514	43	18
	a6	493	100	20.28	3,985	2,586	45	20
au	a1	1,140	0	0	705	210	42	16
	a2	1,143	0	0	577	161	44	29
	a3	1,068	0	0	933	272	45	115
	a4	1,113	0	0	697	177	42	17
	a5	1,090	0	0	924	214	44	23
	a6	1,172	3	0.25	921	235	44	24
hk	a1	21,002	81	0.38	448	304	42	21
	a2	20,944	11	0.05	388	321	44	33
	a3	21,130	729	3.45	573	346	43	18
	a4	21,255	125	0.58	440	286	43	20
	a5	21,091	743	3.52	575	349	44	20
	a6	20,830	807	3.87	570	348	43	20
tw	a1	2,470	0	0	902	294	44	22
	a2	2,877	1	0.03	791	315	44	40
	a3	2,218	0	0	1,155	355	44	17
	a4	2,612	5	0.19	899	300	43	20
	a5	2,339	0	0	1,144	370	44	21
	a6	2,647	1	0.03	1,150	363	45	23
sg	a1	1,895	0	0	561	353	44	19
	a2	1,120	0	0	503	322	43	33
	a3	1,511	0	0	638	409	43	20
	a4	1,643	0	0	509	240	44	15
	a5	1,635	0	0	638	310	44	24
	a6	1,615	0	0	650	308	43	16
us	a1	3,725	0	0	74	135	42	18
	a2	3,578	0	0	317	224	43	33
	a3	3,766	0	0	298	271	43	16
	a4	3,591	0	0	239	260	43	19
	a5	3,933	0	0	433	222	44	30
	a6	3,614	0	0	293	260	44	19

(time duration between the Web service server receiving and requesting and sending out the corresponding response).

The experimental results in Table 3.2 and Fig. 3.2 show:

- As shown in Fig. 3.2a, the response-time (RTT) performance of the target Web services changes dramatically from user to user. For example, invoking Web service "a1" only needs 74 milliseconds on average from the user location of

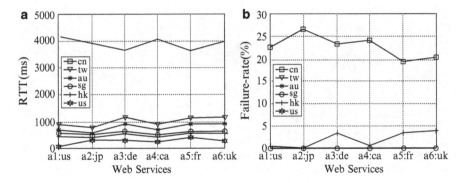

Fig. 3.2 (**a**) Response-time and (**b**) failure-rate performance

"us," while it requires 4,184 milliseconds on average from the user location of "cn."

- As indicated by the SD values in Table 3.2, even in the same location, the RTT performance varies drastically from time to time. For example, in the user location of "cn," the RTT values of invoking "a1" vary from 562 milliseconds to 9,906 milliseconds in our experiment. The unstable RTT performance degrades service quality and makes the latency-sensitive applications easily fail.
- The ProT values in Table 3.2 indicate that the response times of the Amazon Web services mainly consist of network latency rather than server processing time. Since the average process times of all the six Amazon Web services are all less than 50 milliseconds, this is very small compared with the RTT values shown in Table 3.2.
- Users under poor network conditions are more likely to suffer from unreliable service, since unstable RTT performance degrades service quality and even leads to timeout failures. Figure 3.2b, which illustrates the failure probability of the Web services, shows that the service user with the worst RTT performance (i.e., cn) has the highest failure probability, while the service user with the best RTT performance (i.e., us) has the lowest failure probability.

3.4   Evaluation 2: Internet Web Services

This section presents our distributed QoS evaluation results for a large number of real-world Web services. The detailed experimental raw data (e.g., Web service requests, lists of service users and Web services, Web service invocation results) are freely provided online[4] for future research.

---

[4]http://www.wsdream.net

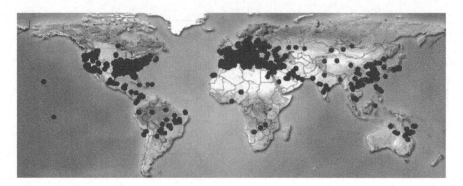

Fig. 3.3 Locations of Web services

3.4.1   Information of Web Services

3.4.1.1   Crawling Web Service Information

Web services can be discovered from UDDI (Universal Description, Discovery, and Integration, which is an XML-based registry enabling companies to publish and discover Web services on the Internet), Web service portals (e.g., *xmethods.net, Webservicex.net, Webservicelist.com*), and Web service search engines [9] (e.g., *seekda.com, esynaps.com*). By crawling Web service information with these mechanisms in Aug. 2009, we obtained 21,358 addresses of WSDL (Web Service Description Language) files, which provided XML-based descriptions of Web service interfaces. Seekda.com [9] reports that there are in total 28,529 public Web services on the Internet. We believe that the 21,358 Web services in our experiments already cover most of the real-world Web services which are publicly available on the Internet.

By analyzing WSDL files, locations of the Web services can be identified. As shown in Fig. 3.3, these Web services are distributed all over the world, while most Web services are located in North America and Europe. Figure 3.4 shows the number of Web services provided by different countries. As shown in Fig. 3.4, the Web service numbers of different countries follow the heavy-tailed distribution. Most countries provide a small number of Web services, while a small number of countries provide a large number of Web services. Among all the 89 countries, the top three countries provide 55.5% of the 21,358 obtained Web services. These three countries are the United States (8,867 Web services), United Kingdom (1,657 Web services), and Germany (1,246 Web services). More detailed information of Web services (e.g., addresses, locations, provider name) is available in our released datasets.

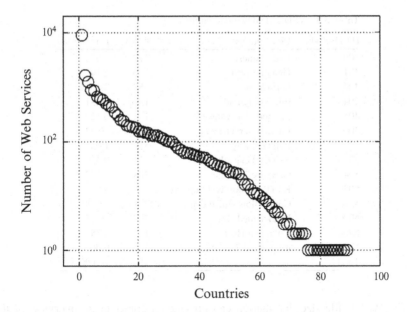

Fig. 3.4 Distribution of Web services

3.4.1.2 Obtaining WSDL Files

By establishing HTTP connections to the 21,358 WSDL addresses obtained in Sect. 3.4.1.1, we successfully downloaded 16,514 (77.32%) WSDL files. The WSDL download failures are summarized in Table 3.3, where the first column lists the HTTP code indicating different types of failures. The HTTP codes of the last four failure types in Table 3.3 are non-available (N/A), since we failed to establish HTTP connections and thus were unable to obtain the server returned HTTP codes. As shown in Table 3.3, there are in total 4,844 failures. 48.49% of these failures are timeout failures caused by network connection problems, including 788 (16.27%) *Gateway Timeout*, 774 (15.98%) *Connection Timed Out*, and 787 (16.25%) *Read Timed Out*. Besides the timeout failures, there are also a lot of *File Not Found* failures (30.31%) and *Internal Server Error* failures (10.43%). The *File Not Found* failures are caused by the removal of WSDL files or updating of WSDL addresses, while the *Internal Server Error* failures are caused by the fact that the servers encountered unexpected conditions which prevented them from fulfilling the request. The various types of WSDL file download failures shown in Table 3.3 indicate that WSDL files on the Internet can become unavailable easily. This high unavailability of WSDL files is caused by the fact that (1) the Internet is highly dynamic and unpredictable, (2) the Web service information on the Internet is out of date, and (3) many Web services are made for experimental purposes.

Table 3.3 WSDL file download failures

HTTP Code	Descriptions	# WS	Percent (%)
400	Bad Request	173	3.57
401	Unauthorized	106	2.19
403	Forbidden	153	3.16
404	File Not Found	1,468	30.31
405	Method Not Allowed	1	0.02
500	Internal Server Error	505	10.43
502	Bad Gateway	51	1.05
503	Service Unavailable	22	0.45
504	Gateway Timeout	788	16.27
505	HTTP Version Not Support	1	0.02
N/A	Connection Timed Out	774	15.98
N/A	Read Timed Out	787	16.25
N/A	Unknown Host	12	0.25
N/A	Redirected Too Many Times	3	0.06
Total		4,844	100.00

The WSDL file size distribution can provide an approximate overview of the current status of real-world WSDL files. To achieve this task, we calculate the sizes of the 16,514 downloaded WSDL files and plot the histogram of the WSDL file size distribution in Fig. 3.5. The average size of the obtained WSDL files is 21.981 KBytes. As shown in Fig. 3.5, 90.5% of WSDL files are between 2 KBytes and 64 KBytes in size, while there are only 676 WSDL files smaller than 2 KBytes and 883 WSDL files larger than 64 KBytes in size.

Although Web services are black box to service users without any internal design and implementation details, we can determine their development technologies by analyzing URLs of the WSDL files. For example, WSDL documents generated by Microsoft .NET usually end with ".*asmx?WSDL.*" We found out that the majority of the collected 16,514 Web services are implemented by Microsoft .NET technology. As shown in Fig. 3.6, 67% of the Web services are implemented by Microsoft .NET technology, 3% are developed by PHP technology, and 30% are implemented by Java and other technologies.

3.4.2   Generating Java Codes for Web Services

Employing Axis2,[5] we successfully generated client-side Web service invocation Java codes for 13,108 (79.38%) Web services among all the 16,514 Web services. In total 235,262,555 lines of Java codes are produced. There are 3,406 code generation failures, which are summarized in Table 3.4. As shown in Table 3.4, among all the

---

[5]http://ws.apache.org/axis2

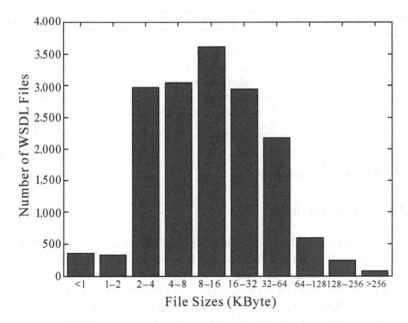

Fig. 3.5 Distribution of WSDL file sizes

Fig. 3.6 Development
technologies

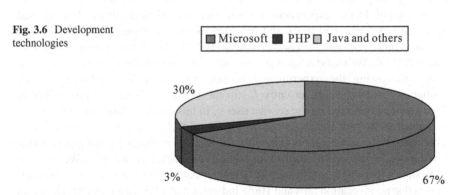

3,406 generation failures, 249 *empty file* failures are caused by the fact that the
obtained WSDL files are empty, 1,232 *invalid file format* failures are due to the
fact that these WSDL files do not follow standard WSDL format, and 1,135 *error
parsing* failures are caused by the syntax errors of the WSDL files. There are also 22
Null QName failures and 4 *databinding unmatched type* failures. These generation
failures indicate that the WSDL files on the Internet are fragile, which may contain
empty content, invalid formats, invalid syntaxes, and other various types of errors.

Table 3.4 Java code
generation failures

Failure Type	# WS	Percent (%)
Empty file	249	7.31
Invalid file format	1,232	36.17
Error parsing WSDL	1,135	33.32
Invocation target exception	764	22.43
Null QName	22	0.65
Databinding unmatched type exception	4	0.12
Total	3,406	100

3.4.3 Failure Probability

3.4.3.1 Dataset Description

To provide objective evaluations of failure probability of the real-world Web services, we randomly select 100 Web services from the 13,108 Web services obtained in Sect. 3.4.2 without any personal selection judgments. To conduct distributed evaluations of the selected Web services, we employed 150 computers in 24 countries from PlanetLab [6], which is a distributed test-bed made up of computers all over the world. To make our Web service evaluation reproducible, Axis2 was employed for generating client-side Web service invocation codes and test cases automatically. In this experiment, each service user invoked all the 100 selected Web services about 100 times and recorded the nonfunctional performance (i.e., response time, response data size, response HTTP code, failure message, etc.). In total 1,542,884 Web service invocation results were collected from the service users.

By processing the experimental results, we obtained a 100×150 failure probability matrix, where an entry $f_{a,i}$ in the matrix is the failure probability of Web service i observed by the service user a. In this chapter, failure probability $f_{a,i}$ is defined as the probability that an invocation on Web service i by user a will fail. The value of $f_{a,i}$ can be approximately calculated by dividing the number of failed invocations by the total number of invocations conducted by user a on Web service i. As shown in Table 3.5, the range of failure probability is from 0 to 100%, where 0 means that no invocation fails and 100% indicates that all invocations fail. The mean and standard deviation of all the 15,000 failure probabilities observed by 100 users on 150 Web services are 4.05 and 17.32%, respectively, indicating that the failure probabilities of different Web services observed by different service users exhibit a great variation. Figure 3.7 shows the value distribution of failure probabilities. As shown in Fig. 3.7, although 85.68% of all the failure probability values are smaller than 1%, a large part (8.34%) of failure probabilities still encounter poor performance with values larger than 16%.

To provide a more comprehensive illustration of the Web service failure probabilities observed by different service users, we randomly selected three service users (user 1 in the USA, user 2 in Finland, and user 3 in Germany) from the 150 service users in this experiment and plotted their observed failure probabilities of the 100 Web services in Fig. 3.8. As shown in Fig. 3.8, these service users have quite different usage experience on the same Web services. Failure probabilities

Table 3.5 Statistics
of dataset 1

Statistics	Values
Num. of Web service invocations	1,542,884
Num. of service users	150
Num. of Web services	100
Num. of user countries	24
Num. of Web service countries	22
Range of failure probability	0–100%
Mean of failure probability	4.05%
Standard deviation of failure probability	17.32%

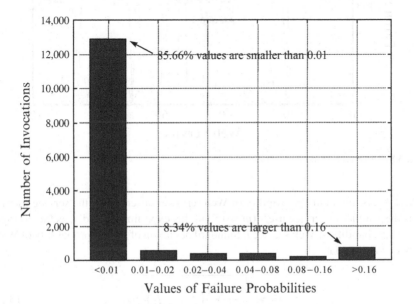

Fig. 3.7 Distributions of failure probabilities

of user 1, user 2, and user 3 are around 40%, 10%, and 0 on most of the Web services. The high failure probability of user 1 is caused by the poor client-side network condition. This experimental observation indicates that different users may have quite different usage experiences on the same Web services, influenced by the network connections.

3.4.3.2   Overall Failure Probability

To investigate the overall failure probabilities of different Web services, the mean of failure probability of Web service i is calculated by

$$\overline{f}_i = \frac{1}{m}\sum_{a=1}^{m} f_{a,i}, \tag{3.1}$$

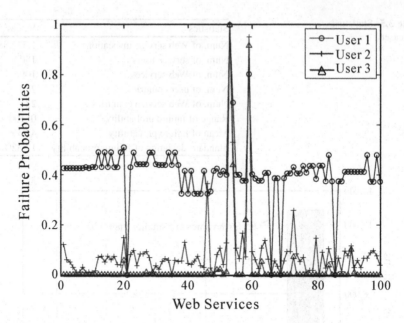

Fig. 3.8 Three users' failure probabilities

where $f_{a,i}$ is the failure probability of Web service i observed by the service user a, m is the number of service users ($m = 150$ in this experiment), and $\overline{f_i}$ is the average failure probability of Web service i. Standard deviation of failure probability of Web service i is calculated by

$$s_i = \sqrt{\frac{1}{m} \sum_{a=1}^{m} \left(f_{a,i} - \overline{f_i} \right)^2},$$ (3.2)

where $\overline{f_i}$ is the average failure probability of Web service i and s_i is the standard deviation of failure probability of Web service i.

Similarly, the average failure probability of a service user a can be calculated by

$$\overline{f_a} = \frac{1}{n} \sum_{i=1}^{n} f_{a,i},$$ (3.3)

where n is the number of Web services ($n = 100$ in this experiment) and $\overline{f_a}$ is the mean of service user a. Standard deviation of failure probability of service user a can be calculated by

$$s_a = \sqrt{\frac{1}{n} \sum_{i=1}^{n} \left(f_{a,i} - \overline{f_a} \right)^2},$$ (3.4)

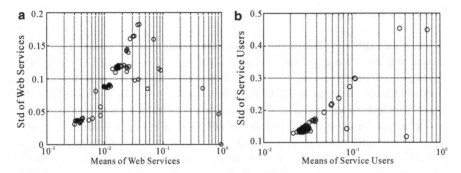

Fig. 3.9 Average failure probabilities

where $\overline{f_a}$ is the mean of service user a and s_a is the standard deviation of service user a.

Figures 3.9a, b show the mean and standard deviation of the 100 Web services and 150 service users, respectively, where the x-axis of the figure is the mean value and the y-axis is the standard deviation value. Figure 3.9a shows that (1) average failure probabilities of all of the 100 Web services are larger than 0, indicating that a 100% invocation success rate is very difficult to achieve in the unpredictable Internet environment, since Web service invocation failures can be caused by client-side errors, network errors, or server-side errors. (2) The standard deviation first becomes larger with the increase in the mean and begins to decrease after a certain threshold. This is because the Web services with very large average failure probabilities are usually caused by server-side errors. The value variation of these Web services to different users is thus not large. For example, there is a Web service with 100% failure probability (caused by the unavailability of that Web service) in Fig. 3.9a. The standard deviation of this Web service is 0, since all the users obtained the same failure probability, that is, 100%. (3) Although average failure probabilities of most Web services are small, the standard deviations are quite large, indicating that failure probability values of the same Web service observed by different service users can vary widely.

Figure 3.9b shows that (1) average failure probabilities of all of the 150 service users are all larger than 0, although they are in different locations under various network conditions. This observation indicates that Web service invocation failures are difficult to avoid in the Internet environment. (2) There is an outlier in Fig. 3.9b which has a large mean value (0.412) and very small standard deviation value (0.12). This is because most failures (i.e., *UnknownHostException*) of this service user happen to all the other Web services, making the observed failure probabilities on different Web services quite similar. (3) Although average failure probabilities of most service users are small, the standard deviations of most of them are quite large, indicating that the failure probabilities of different Web services observed by the same service user are also quite different.

3.4.3.3   Failure Types

To investigate different Web service invocation failures, HTTP codes of the Web service responses are employed for the failure detection (i.e., HTTP code 200 indicates invocation success, while other codes and exceptions stand for various types of failures). In some special cases, Web service responses with HTTP code 200 may include functional failure information (e.g., invalid parameter). Such Web service invocations are considered successful, since the target Web services are operating correctly. Since this chapter only focuses on nonfunctional performance evaluation, functional testing of Web services is not considered. As shown in Table 3.6, among all the 1,542,884 Web service invocations, there are 58,184 invocation failures. The detailed failures information is summarized in Table 3.6, and descriptions of different failure types are introduced as follows:

- *(400)Bad Request*: The Web server was unable to understand the request since the client request did not respect the HTTP protocol completely.
- *(500)Internal Server Error*: The Web server encountered an unexpected condition that prevented it from fulfilling the client request.
- *(502)Bad Gateway*: A gateway or proxy server received an invalid response from an upstream server it accessed to fulfill the request.
- *(503)Service Unavailable*: The Web server was unable to handle the HTTP request due to temporary overloading or maintenance of the server.
- *Network Is Unreachable*: A socket operation was attempted to an unreachable network. It did not get a response, and there was no default gateway.
- *Connection Reset*: The socket was closed unexpectedly from the server side.
- *NoRoutetoHostException*: Socket connection failed caused by intervening firewall or intermediate router errors.
- *Connection Refused*: An error occurred while attempting to connect a socket to a remote address and port. Typically, the connection was refused remotely (e.g., no process was listening on the remote address/port).
- *Read Timed Out*: Timeout occurred on socket read.
- *UnknownHostException*: The IP address of a host could not be determined.
- *Connect Timed Out*: A timeout has occurred on a socket connect.
- *Other Failures*: The type of these invocation failures cannot be identified due to lack of failure information.

As shown in Table 3.6, about 85% of these failures are due to socket connection problems, including 44,809 *Connect Timed Out* and 4,606 *Read Timed Out*. These timed out exceptions are caused by network connection problems during socket connection and socket read. In this experiment, all Web service invocations are configured with a timeout of 20 s, which is the default setting of Axis2. By setting a larger timeout value, the number of invocation failures may decrease. The investigations of invocation timeout settings will be conducted in our future work. Besides the timeout exceptions, there are also a lot of other failures caused by network errors, including 33 *Bad Gateway*, 3 *Network Is Unreachable*, 415 *No*

Table 3.6 Failures of dataset 1

Failure types	Number
(400)Bad Request	3
(500)Internal Server Error	26
(502)Bad Gateway	33
(503)Service Unavailable	609
java.net.SocketException: Network Is Unreachable	3
java.net.SocketException: Connection Reset	1,175
java.net.NoRouteToHostException: No Route to Host	415
java.net.ConnectException: Connection Refused	619
java.net.SocketTimeoutException: Read Timed Out	4,606
java.net.UnknownHostException	5,847
java.net.SocketTimeoutException: Connect Timed Out	44,809
Other errors	39
Total	58,184

Route to Host, and 5,847 *Unknown Host*. These failures together with the timeout failures account for a large percentage (95.5%) of the Web service invocation failures, indicating that the Web service invocation failures are mainly caused by network errors. Some failures in Table 3.6 are caused by server-side errors, including 3 *Bad Request*, 26 *Internal Server Error*, 608 *Service Unavailable*, 1,175 *Connection Reset*, and 619 *Connection Refused*. Compared with the failures caused by network errors, the number of failures caused by server-side errors is very small.

These experimental observations of invocation failures show us that (1) Web service invocations can fail easily, which can be caused by gateway errors, networking errors, and server errors. (2) In the service-oriented environment, providing reliable Web services is not enough for building reliable service-oriented systems, since most invocation failures are caused by network errors. (3) Since the Web service invocation failures are unavoidable in the unpredictable Internet environment, service fault tolerance approaches [11, 18] are becoming important for building reliable service-oriented systems. (4) To tolerate invocation failures caused by network errors, service fault tolerance mechanisms should be developed at the client side.

3.4.4   Response Time and Throughput

3.4.4.1   Dataset Description

This experiment focuses on investigating the response time and throughput of different Web services and service users. Response time is defined as the time duration between a service user sending a request and receiving the corresponding response, while throughput is defined as the average rate of successful message size (here in bits) delivery over a communication channel per second. This experiment

Table 3.7 Statistics of the dataset 2

Statistics	Values
Num. of Web service invocations	1,974,675
Num. of service users	339
Num. of Web services	5,825
Num. of user countries	30
Num. of Web service countries	73
Mean of response time	1.43 s
Standard deviation of response time	31.9 s
Mean of throughput	102.86 kbps
Standard deviation of throughput	531.85 kbps

was conducted in Aug. 2009. As shown in Table 3.7, in total 1,974,675 real-world Web service invocations were executed by 339 service users from 30 countries on 5,825 real-world Web services from 73 countries in this experiment.

By processing the Web service invocation results, we obtained two $339 \times 5,825$ matrices for response time and throughput, respectively. Each entry in a matrix represents the response time or throughput value observed by a user on a Web service. As shown in Table 3.7, the mean and standard deviation of response time were 1.43 and 31.9 s, respectively, while the mean and standard deviation of throughput were 102.86 and 531.85 kbps, respectively.

3.4.4.2 Overall Response Time and Throughput

Figures 3.10a, b show the overall response time of Web services and service users, respectively. From Fig. 3.10a, we observe that (1) Web services with a large average response time tend to have large performance variance for different users, since the standard deviation increases with the mean value in Fig. 3.10a. (2) Large response of a Web service can be caused by the long data transfer time or the long request processing time at the server side. For example, the largest response time (1,535 s) shown in Fig. 3.10a is mainly caused by large size data transfer (12 MB data are transferred), while the response time of the outlier (mean = 5.3 s, SD = 0.0003) in Fig. 3.10a is mainly caused by the long request processing time on the server side. When the response time of a Web service is mainly due to the server-side processing time, different users will receive a similar response time, and the standard deviation value will thus be small.

Figure 3.10b shows that (1) service users with a large response time are more likely to observe greater response time variance on different Web services, since the standard deviation increases with the mean value in Fig. 3.10b. (2) Influenced by the client-side network conditions, different service users observe quite different average response times for the same Web services. Although most service users get a good average response time, there are still a small number of service users that receive a very large average response time.

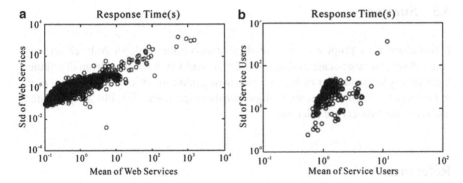

Fig. 3.10 Overall response time

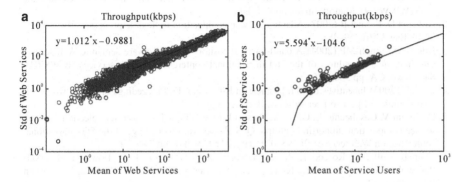

Fig. 3.11 Overall throughput

Figures 3.11a, b show the overall throughput value of different Web services and service users, respectively. Figure 3.11a shows that (1) similar to the response time, standard deviation of throughput increases with the mean value. (2) Influenced by the poor server-side network conditions, there is a small part of Web services providing a very poor average throughput (<1 kbps). Figure 3.11b shows that (1) influenced by the client-side network conditions, different service users receive quite different average throughput on the target Web services. (2) Service users with large average throughput values are more likely to observe large throughput variance for different Web services, since the standard deviation increases with the mean value.

In Figs. 3.11a, b, two linear functions are fitted to the observed value points. Their equations are also provided. From these equations, performance variance of a Web service (or a service user) can be predicted by their throughput values.

3.5 Summary

In this chapter, we propose a distributed evaluation framework for Web services and conduct several large-scale evaluations of real-world Web services from distributed locations. A large number of Web service invocations are executed by service users in heterogeneous environments. Comprehensive experimental results are presented, and reusable datasets are released.

References

1. Alrifai M, Risse T (2009) Combining global optimization with local selection for efficient QoS-aware service composition. In: Proceedings of the 18th international conference on World Wide Web (WWW'09), Madrid, Spain, pp 881–890
2. Ardagna D, Pernici B (2007) Adaptive service composition in flexible processes. IEEE Trans Softw Eng 33(6):369–384
3. Bilgin AS, Singh MP (2004) A daml-based repository for QoS-aware semantic Web service selection. In: Proceedings of the 2nd international conference on Web services (ICWS'04), San Diego, CA, pp 368–375
4. Bram C (2003) Incentives build robustness in BitTorrent. In: Proceedings of the 1st workshop on economics of peer-to-peer systems, Berkeley, CA, pp 1–5
5. Cardellini V, Casalicchio E, Grassi V, Presti FL (2007) Flow-based service selection for Web service composition supporting multiple QoS classes. In: Proceedings of the 5th international conference on Web services (ICWS'07), Salt Lake City, UT, pp 743–750
6. Chun B, Culler D, Roscoe T, Bavier A, Peterson L, Wawrzoniak M, Bowman M (2003) Planetlab: an overlay testbed for broad-coverage services. ACM SIGCOMM Comput Commun Rev 33(3):3–12
7. Fang CL, Liang D, Lin F, Lin CC (2007) Fault-tolerant Web services. J Syst Architect 53(1):21–38
8. Haddad JE, Manouvrier M, Ramirez G, Rukoz M (2008) QoS-driven selection of Web services for transactional composition. In: Proceedings of the 6th international conference on Web services (ICWS'08), Beijing, China, pp 653–660
9. Lausen H, Haselwanter T (2007) Finding Web services. In: Proceedings of the 1st European semantic technology conference, Vienna, Austria
10. Menasce DA (2002) QoS issues in Web services. IEEE Internet Comput 6(6):72–75
11. Salatge N, Fabre JC (2007) Fault tolerance connectors for unreliable Web services. In: Proceedings of the 37th international conference on dependable systems and networks (DSN'07), Edinburgh, UK, pp 51–60
12. Wu G, Wei J, Qiao X, Li L (2007) A Bayesian network based QoS assessment model for Web services. In: Proceedings of the international conference on services computing (SCC'07), Salt Lake City, UT, pp 498–505
13. Yu T, Zhang Y, Lin KJ (2007) Efficient algorithms for Web services selection with end-to-end QoS constraints. ACM Trans Web 1(1):1–26
14. Zeng L, Benatallah B, Ngu AH, Dumas M, Kalagnanam J, Chang H (2004) Qos-aware middleware for Web services composition. IEEE Trans Softw Eng 30(5):311–327
15. Zhang LJ, Zhang J, Cai H (2007) Services computing. Springer/Tsinghua University Press, Berlin/Beijing
16. Zheng Z, Lyu MR (2008) A distributed replication strategy evaluation and selection framework for fault-tolerant Web services. In: Proceedings of the 6th international conference Web services (ICWS'08), Beijing, China, pp 145–152

17. Zheng Z, Lyu MR (2008) WS-DREAM: a distributed reliability assessment mechanism for Web services. In: Proceedings of the 38th international conference on dependable systems and networks (DSN'08), Anchorage, Alaska, USA, pp 392–397

18. Zheng Z, Lyu MR (2009) A QoS-aware fault tolerant middleware for dependable service composition. In: Proceedings of the 39th international conference on dependable systems and networks (DSN'09), Lisbon, Portugal, pp 239–248

19. Zheng Z, Lyu MR (2010) Collaborative reliability prediction for service-oriented systems. In: Proceedings of the IEEE/ACM 32nd international conference on software engineering (ICSE'10), Cape Town, South Africa, pp 35–44

20. Zheng Z, Ma H, Lyu MR, King I (2009) WSRec: a collaborative filtering based Web service recommender system. In: Proceedings of the 7th international conference on Web services (ICWS'09), Los Angeles, CA, pp 437–444

Chapter 4
Neighborhood-Based QoS Prediction of Web Services

Abstract To accurately predict the Web service QoS values, this chapter proposes a neighborhood-based collaborative filtering approach for predicting the QoS values for the current user by employing historical Web service QoS data from other similar users. The proposed approach systematically combines the user-based approach and the item-based approach. Our approach requires no Web service invocations and can help service users discover suitable Web services by analyzing QoS information from their similar users.

Keywords QoS prediction • Neighborhood-based prediction • Collaborative filtering • Service invocation

4.1 Overview

With the number of Web services increasing, quality of service (QoS) is usually employed for describing nonfunctional characteristics of Web services [14]. Among different QoS properties of Web services, some QoS properties are user dependent and have different values for different users (e.g., *response time, invocation failure probability*). Obtaining values of the user-dependent QoS properties is a challenging task. Real-world Web service evaluation on the client side [3, 11, 15] is usually required for measuring performance of the user-dependent QoS properties of Web services. Client-side Web service evaluation requires real-world Web service invocations and encounters the following drawbacks:

- Firstly, real-world Web service invocations impose costs for the service users and consume resources of the service providers. Some Web service invocations may even be charged.
- Secondly, there may be too many Web service candidates to be evaluated, and some suitable Web services may not be discovered and included in the evaluation list by the service users.

Z. Zheng and M.R. Lyu, *QoS Management of Web Services*, Advanced Topics in Science and Technology in China, DOI 10.1007/978-3-642-34207-3_4, © Zhejiang University Press, Hangzhou and Springer-Verlag Berlin Heidelberg 2013

- Finally, most service users are not experts on Web service evaluation, and the common time-to-market constraints limit an in-depth evaluation of the target Web services.

However, without sufficient client-side evaluation, accurate values of the user-dependent QoS properties cannot be obtained. Optimal Web service selection and recommendation are thus difficult to achieve. To attack this critical challenge, we propose a neighborhood-based collaborative filtering approach for making personalized QoS value prediction for the service users. Collaborative filtering [5] is the method which automatically predicts values of the current user by collecting information from other similar users or items. Well-known neighborhood-based collaborative filtering methods include user-based approaches [1, 6, 12] and item-based approaches [4, 7, 9]. Due to their great successes in modeling characteristics of users and items, collaborative filtering techniques have been widely employed in famous commercial systems, such as Amazon[1] and eBay.[2] In this chapter, we systematically combine the user-based approach and item-based approach for predicting the QoS values for the current user by employing historical Web service QoS data from other similar users and similar Web services. Similar service users are defined as the service users who have similar historical QoS experience of the same set of commonly invoked Web services with the current user.

Different from traditional Web service evaluation approaches [3, 11, 15], our approach predicts user-dependent QoS values of the target Web services without requiring real-world Web service invocations. The Web service QoS values obtained by our approach can be employed by other QoS driven approaches (e.g., Web service selection [13, 14], fault-tolerant Web service [16]).

The rest of this chapter is organized as follows. Section 4.2 introduces a user-collaborative QoS data collection mechanism. Section 4.3 presents the similarity computation method. Section 4.4 proposes a Web service QoS value prediction approach. Section 4.5 shows the implementation and experiments. Section 4.6 concludes this chapter.

4.2 User-Collaborative QoS Collection

To make accurate QoS value prediction of Web services without real-world Web service invocations, we need to collect past Web service QoS information from other service users. However, it is difficult to collect Web service QoS information from different service users because (1) Web services are distributed over the Internet and are hosted by different organizations, (2) service users are usually isolated from each other, and (3) the current Web service architecture does not provide any mechanism for Web service QoS information sharing.

---

[1]http://www.amazon.com

[2]http://www.half.ebay.com

Fig. 4.1 Procedures of QoS
value prediction

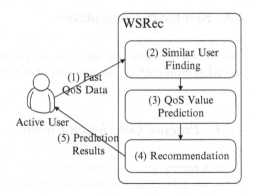

Inspired by the recent success of *YouTube*[3] and *Wikipedia*,[4] we propose the concept of *user collaboration* for Web service QoS information sharing between service users. The idea is that, instead of contributing videos (*YouTube*) or knowledge (*Wikipedia*), the service users are encouraged to contribute their individually observed past Web service QoS data. Figure 4.1 shows the procedures of our user-collaborative QoS data collection mechanism, which are introduced as follows:

1. A service user contributes past Web service QoS data to a centralized server WSRec [17]. In the rest of this chapter, the service users who require QoS value prediction services are named as *active users*.
2. WSRec selects similar users to the training users for the active users (technique details will be introduced in Sect. 4.3). *Training users* represent the service users whose QoS values are stored in the WSRec server and employed for making value predictions for the active users.
3. WSRec predicts QoS values of Web services for the active users (technique details will be introduced in Sect. 4.4).
4. WSRec makes Web service recommendation based on the predicted QoS values of different Web services (will be discussed in Sect. 4.4.4).
5. The service user receives the predicted QoS values as well as the recommendation results, which can be employed to assist decision making (e.g., service selection, composite service performance prediction).

In our user-collective mechanism, the active users who contribute more Web service QoS data will obtain more accurate QoS value predictions (details will be explained in Sect. 4.4). By this method, the service users are encouraged to contribute their past Web service QoS data. More architecture and implementation details of WSRec will be introduced in Sect. 4.5.1.

---

[3]http://www.youtube.com

[4]http://www.wikipedia.org

4.3 Similarity Computation

This section introduces the similarity computation method of different service users as well as different Web services (step 2 of Fig. 4.1).

4.3.1 Pearson Correlation Coefficient

Given a recommender system consisting of M training users and N Web service items, the relationship between service users and Web service items is denoted by an $M \times N$ matrix, called the user-item matrix. Every entry in this matrix $r_{u,i}$ represents a vector of QoS values (e.g., response time, failure probability) that is observed by the service user u on the Web service item i. If user u did not invoke the Web service item i before, then $r_{u,i} = $ null. In the case that a Web service includes multiple operations, each item (column) of the user-item matrix represents a Web service operation instead of a Web service.

The Pearson Correlation Coefficient (PCC) has been introduced in a number of recommender systems for similarity computation, since it can be easily implemented and can achieve high accuracy. In user-based collaborative filtering methods for Web services, PCC is employed to calculate the similarity between two service users a and u based on the Web service items they commonly invoked, using the following equation:

$$\text{Sim}(a, u) = \frac{\sum_{i \in I} (r_{a,i} - \bar{r}_a)(r_{u,i} - \bar{r}_u)}{\sqrt{\sum_{i \in I} (r_{a,i} - \bar{r}_a)^2} \sqrt{\sum_{i \in I} (r_{u,i} - \bar{r}_u)^2}}, \tag{4.1}$$

where $I = I_a \cap I_u$ is the subset of Web service items which both user a and user u have invoked previously, $r_{a,i}$ is a vector of QoS values of Web service item i observed by service user a, and $\bar{r}_a$ and $\bar{r}_u$ represent average QoS values of different Web services observed by service users a and u, respectively. From this definition, the similarity of two service users, Sim (a, u), is in the interval of $[-1, 1]$, where a larger PCC value indicates that service users a and u are more similar. When two service users have null Web service intersection ($I = $ null), the value of Sim (a, u) cannot be determined (Sim $(a, u) = $ null), since we do not have information for the similarity computation.

Item-based collaborative filtering methods using PCC [4, 9] are similar to the user-based methods. The difference is that item-based methods employ the similarity between the Web service items instead of the service users. The similarity computation of two Web service items i and j can be calculated by

$$\text{Sim}(i, j) = \frac{\sum\limits_{u \in U} (r_{u,i} - \overline{r}_i)(r_{u,j} - \overline{r}_j)}{\sqrt{\sum\limits_{u \in U} (r_{u,i} - \overline{r}_i)^2} \sqrt{\sum\limits_{u \in U} (r_{u,j} - \overline{r}_j)^2}}, \tag{4.2}$$

where Sim (i, j) is the similarity between Web service items i and j, $U = U_i \cap U_j$ is the subset of service users who have invoked both Web service item i and Web service item j previously, and $\overline{r}_i$ represents the average QoS values of the Web service item i observed by different service users. Sim (i, j) is also in the interval of $[-1, 1]$. When two Web service items have null service user intersection ($U =$ null), the value of Sim (i, j) cannot be computed (Sim $(i, j) =$ null).

4.3.2 Significance Weighting

Although PCC can provide accurate similarity computation, it will overestimate the similarities of service users who are actually not similar but happen to have similar QoS experience on a few co-invoked Web services [8]. To address this problem, we employ a *significance weight* to reduce the influence of a small number of similar co-invoked items. An enhanced PCC for the similarity computation between different service users is defined as

$$\text{Sim}'(a, u) = \frac{2 \times |I_a \cap I_u|}{|I_a| + |I_u|} \text{Sim}(a, u), \tag{4.3}$$

where Sim$'(a, u)$ is the new similarity value, $|I_a \cap I_u|$ is the number of Web service items that are employed by both the two users, and $|I_a|$ and $|I_u|$ are the number of Web services invoked by user a and user u, respectively. When the co-invoked Web service number $|I_a \cap I_u|$ is small, the *significance weight* $\frac{2 \times |I_a \cap I_u|}{|I_a| + |I_u|}$ will decrease the similarity estimation between the service users a and u. Since the value of $\frac{2 \times |I_a \cap I_u|}{|I_a| + |I_u|}$ is between the interval of $[0, 1]$ and the value Sim (a, u) is in the interval of $[-1, 1]$, the value of Sim$'(a, u)$ is in the interval of $[-1, 1]$.

Just like the user-based methods, an enhanced PCC for the similarity computation between different Web service items is defined as

$$\text{Sim}'(i, j) = \frac{2 \times |U_i \cap U_j|}{|U_i| + |U_j|} \text{Sim}(i, j), \tag{4.4}$$

where $|U_i \cap U_j|$ is the number of service users who invoked both Web service item i and item j previously. Similar to Sim$'(a, u)$, the value of Sim$'(i, j)$ is also in the interval of $[-1, 1]$.

As will be shown in our experimental results in Sect. 4.5.5, the *similarity weight* enhances the QoS value prediction accuracy of Web services. Based on the above similarity computation approach, if an active user provides more past QoS values of Web services to WSRec, the similarities computation will be more accurate, which will consequently improve the QoS value prediction accuracy. In this way, the service users are encouraged to provide more Web service QoS data.

4.4 QoS Value Prediction

In reality, the user-item matrix is usually very sparse [9], which will greatly influence the prediction accuracy. Predicting missing values for the user-item matrix can improve the prediction accuracy of active users [10]. Consequently, we propose a missing value prediction approach for making the matrix denser. The similar users or items of a missing value in the user-item matrix will be employed for predicting the value. By this approach, the user-item matrix becomes denser. This enhanced user-item matrix will be employed for the missing value prediction for the active users.

4.4.1 Similar Neighbors Selection

Before predicting the missing values in the user-item matrix, the similar neighbors of an entry, which include a set of similar users and a set of similar items, need to be identified. Similar neighbor selection is an important step for making accurate missing value prediction, since dissimilar neighbors will decrease the prediction accuracy. Traditional Top-K algorithms rank the neighbors based on their PCC similarities and select the Top-K most similar neighbors for making missing value prediction. In practice, some entries in the user-item matrix have limited similar neighbors or even do not have any neighbors. Traditional Top-K algorithms ignore this problem and still include dissimilar neighbors to predict the missing value, which will greatly reduce the prediction accuracy. To attack this problem, we propose an enhanced Top-K algorithm, where neighbors with PCC similarities smaller or equal to 0 will be excluded.

To predict a missing value $r_{u,i}$ in the user-item matrix, a set of similar users $S(u)$ can be found by the following equation:

$$S(u) = \{u_a | u_a \in T(u), \text{Sim}'(u_a, u) > 0, u_a \neq u\}, \tag{4.5}$$

and a set of similar Web service items $S(i)$ can be found by the following equation:

$$S(i) = \{i_k | i_k \in T(i), \text{Sim}'(i_k, i) > 0, i_k \neq i\}, \tag{4.6}$$

where $T(u)$ is a set of Top-K similar users to the user u and $T(i)$ is a set of Top-K similar items to the item i. In this way, the null intersection neighbors and the dissimilar neighbors with negative correlations will be discarded from the similar neighbor sets.

4.4.2 Missing Value Prediction

User-based collaborative filtering methods [1] (named as UPCC for ease of presentation) apply similar users to predict the missing QoS values by the following equation:

$$
P\left(r_{u,i}\right) = \bar{u} + \frac{\sum\limits_{u_a \in S(u)} \text{Sim}'\left(u_a, u\right)\left(r_{u_a,i} - \bar{u}_a\right)}{\sum\limits_{u_a \in S(u)} \text{Sim}'\left(u_a, u\right)}, \tag{4.7}
$$

where $P(r_{u,i})$ is a vector of predicted QoS values of the missing value $r_{u,i}$ in the user-item matrix, $\bar{u}$ is a vector of average QoS values of different Web services observed by the active user u, and $\bar{u}_a$ is a vector of average QoS values of different Web services observed by the similar service user u_a.

Similar to user-based methods, item-based collaborative filtering methods [9] (named as IPCC) engage similar Web service items to predict the missing value by employing the following equation:

$$
P\left(r_{u,i}\right) = \bar{i} + \frac{\sum\limits_{i_k \in S(i)} \text{Sim}'\left(i_k, i\right)\left(r_{u,i_k} - \bar{i}_k\right)}{\sum\limits_{i_k \in S(i)} \text{Sim}'\left(i_k, i\right)}, \tag{4.8}
$$

where $P(r_{u,i})$ is a vector of predicted QoS values of the entry $r_{u,i}$ and $\bar{i}$ is a vector of average QoS values of Web service item i observed by different service users.

When a missing value does not have similar users, we use the similar items to predict the missing value, and vice versa. When $S(u) \neq \emptyset \wedge S(i) \neq \emptyset$, predicting the missing value only with user-based methods or item-based methods will potentially ignore valuable information that can make the prediction more accurate. In order to predict the missing value as accurately as possible, we systematically combine user-based and item-based methods to fully utilize the information of the similar users and similar items.

Since the user-based method and item-based method may achieve different prediction accuracy, we employ two *confidence weights*, con_u and con_i, to balance the results from these two prediction methods. Confidence weights are calculated by considering the similarities of the similar neighbors. For example, assume a missing value in the user-item matrix has three similar users with PCC similarity $\{1,1,1\}$ and has three similar items with PCC similarity $\{0.1, 0.1, 0.1\}$. In this case, the prediction confidence by the user-based method is much higher than the item-based method, since the similar users have higher similarities (PCC values) compared with the similar items. Consequently, con_u is defined as

$$
\text{con}_u = \sum_{u_a \in S(u)} \frac{\text{Sim}'(u_a, u)}{\sum_{u_a \in S(u)} \text{Sim}'(u_a, u)} \times \text{Sim}'(u_a, u), \tag{4.9}
$$

and con_i is defined as

$$con_i = \sum_{i_k \in S(i)} \frac{Sim'(i_k, i)}{\sum_{i_k \in S(i)} Sim'(i_k, i)} \times Sim'(i_k, i), \qquad (4.10)$$

where con_u and con_i are the prediction confidence of the user-based method and item-based method, respectively, and a higher value indicates a higher confidence of the predicted value $P(r_{u, i})$.

Since different datasets may inherit their own data distribution and correlation characteristics, a parameter λ ($0 \le \lambda \le 1$) is employed to determine how much our QoS value prediction approach relies on the user-based method and the item-based method. When $S(u) \ne \varnothing \wedge S(i) \ne \varnothing$, our method predicts the missing QoS value $r_{u, i}$ by employing the following equation:

$$P(r_{u,i}) = w_u \times \left(\bar{u} + \frac{\sum_{u_a \in S(u)} Sim'(u_a, u) (r_{u_a,i} - \bar{u}_a)}{\sum_{u_a \in S(u)} Sim'(u_a, u)} \right)$$

$$+ w_i \times \left(\bar{i} + \frac{\sum_{i_k \in S(i)} Sim'(i_k, i) (r_{u,i_k} - \bar{i}_k)}{\sum_{i_k \in S(i)} Sim'(i_k, i)} \right), \qquad (4.11)$$

where w_u and w_i are the weights of the user-based method and the item-based method, respectively ($w_u + w_i = 1$). w_u is defined as

$$w_u = \frac{con_u \times \lambda}{con_u \times \lambda + con_i \times (1 - \lambda)}, \qquad (4.12)$$

and w_i is defined as

$$w_i = \frac{con_i \times (1 - \lambda)}{con_u \times \lambda + con_i \times (1 - \lambda)}, \qquad (4.13)$$

where both w_u and w_i are the combinations of the *confidence weights* (con_u and con_i) and the parameter λ. The prediction confidence of the missing value $P(r_{u, i})$ by our approach using Eq. (4.11) can be calculated by equation

$$con = w_u \times con_u + w_i \times con_i. \qquad (4.14)$$

When $S(u) \ne \varnothing \wedge S(i) \ne \varnothing$, since there are no similar items, the missing value prediction degrades to the user-based approach by employing Eq. (4.7), and the confidence of the predicted value is $con = con_u$. Similarly, when $S(u) = \varnothing \wedge S(i) \ne \varnothing$, the missing value prediction relies only on the similar items by employing Eq. (4.8), and the confidence of the predicted value is con $=$ con$_i$. When $S(u) = \varnothing \wedge S(i) = \varnothing$, since there are no similar users or items for the missing value $r_{u,\,i}$, we do not predict the missing value in the user-item matrix. The prediction of $P\,(r_{u,\,i})$ is defined as

$$P(r_{u,i}) = \text{null.} \tag{4.15}$$

By the above design, instead of predicting all the missing values in the user-item training matrix, we only predict the missing values, which have similar users or similar items. The consideration is that no prediction is better than bad prediction, since the user-item matrix will be involved for predicting QoS values for the active users and bad prediction will decrease the prediction accuracy for the active users. We also propose *confidence weights* (con$_u$ and con$_i$) to balance the user-based prediction and the item-based prediction automatically. Moreover, a parameter λ is employed to enhance the feasibility of our method for different datasets. These designs are different from all other existing prediction methods, and the experimental results in Sect. 4.5 show that these designs can significantly enhance the QoS value prediction accuracy of Web services.

4.4.3 Prediction for Active Users

After predicting missing values in the user-item matrix, we apply the matrix for predicting QoS values for active users. The prediction procedures are similar to the missing value prediction in Sect. 4.4.2. The only difference is that when $S(u) = \varnothing \wedge S(i) = \varnothing$, we predict the QoS values by employing the user mean (UMEAN) and item mean (IMEAN), where UMEAN is a vector of average QoS values of different Web services observed by the service user a and IMEAN is a vector of average QoS values of the Web service item i observed by different service users. The prediction formula is defined as

$$P(r_{a,i}) = w_u \times \bar{r}_a + w_i \times \bar{r}_i, \tag{4.16}$$

where $\bar{r}_a$ is the UMEAN and $\bar{r}_i$ is the IMEAN. In this case, the confidence of the predicted value is con $= 0$.

4.4.4 Web Service Recommendation

After predicting the QoS values of Web services for an active user, the predicted QoS values can be employed in the following ways: (1) For a set of functionally equivalent Web services, the optimal one can be selected based on the predicted QoS performance and the prediction confidence. (2) For the Web services with different functionalities, the Top-K best performing Web services can be recommended to the service users to help them discover potentially good performing Web services. (3) The Top-K active service users, who have good predicted QoS values on a Web service, can be recommended to the corresponding service provider to help the provider find its potential customers.

Different from all other existing prediction methods, our method not only provides the predicted QoS values for the active users but also includes the prediction confidences, which can be employed by the service users for better Web service selection.

4.4.5 Computational Complexity Analysis

This section discusses the upper bound of the worst-case computational complexity of the QoS value prediction algorithms. We assume there are m service users and n Web services in the training matrix.

4.4.5.1 Complexity of Similarity Computation

In Sect. 4.3, the computational complexity of $Sim(a, u)$ is $O(n)$, since there are at most n intersecting Web services between service user a and service user u. The computational complexity of $Sim(i, j)$ is $O(m)$, since there are at most m intersecting service users between Web service i and Web service j.

4.4.5.2 Complexity of UPCC

When predicting the missing values for an active user employing the user-based PCC algorithm (Eq. 4.7), we need to compute similarities of the active user with all the m training users in the training matrix (totally m similarity computations). As discussed in Sect. 4.4.5.1, the computational complexity of each similarity computation is $O(n)$. Therefore, the computational complexity of the similarity computation is $O(mn)$.

The computational complexity of each missing value prediction for the active user is $O(m)$, since at most m similar users will be employed for the prediction. There are at most n missing values in an active user, so the computational complexity of the value prediction for an active user is $O(mn)$. Therefore, the total computational complexity of UPCC (including similarity computation and value prediction) is $O(mn)$.

4.4.5.3 Complexity of IPCC

When predicting the missing values for an active Web service employing the item-based PCC algorithm (Eq. 4.8), we need to compute similarities of the current Web service with all the n Web services in the training matrix (totally n similarity computations). As discussed in Sect. 4.4.5.1, the computational complexity of each similarity computation is $O(m)$. Therefore, the computational complexity of the similarity computation is $O(mn)$.

After the similarity computation, for each missing value of an active Web service, the value prediction computational complexity is $O(n)$, since at most n similar Web services will be employed for the value prediction. There are at most m missing values in an active Web service, so the computational complexity of the value prediction for an active Web service is $O(mn)$. Therefore, the same as for UPCC, the computational complexity of IPCC is also $O(mn)$.

4.4.5.4 Complexity of Training Matrix Prediction

In Sect. 4.4.2, we predict the missing values in the training matrix. When employing the UPCC approach, the computational complexity is $O(m^2n)$ since there are at most m rows (users) to be predicted. When employing the IPCC approach, the computational complexity is $O(mn^2)$ because there are at most n columns (Web services) to be predicted.

Since our approach is a linear combination of the UPCC and IPCC approaches, the computational complexity of our approach is s. Because the value prediction for the training matrix can be precomputed and recomputation is required only when the training matrix is updated, it will not influence the real-time prediction performance for active users.

4.4.5.5 Complexity of Active User Prediction

As discussed in Sect. 4.4.5.2, the computational complexity of UPCC for predicting values of an active user is $O(mn)$. When employing IPCC, the similarities of different columns (Web services) can be precomputed, and there are at most n missing values in the active user. For the prediction of each missing value, the computational complexity is $O(n)$, since at most n similar Web services will be employed for the prediction. Therefore, the computational complexity of IPCC for an active user is $O(n^2)$.

Since our QoS value prediction approach is a linear combination of UPCC and IPCC, the computational complexity of our approach for an active user is $O(mn + n^2)$.

4.5 Implementation and Experiments

4.5.1 Implementation

A prototype named WSRec [17] is implemented with JDK, Eclipse, Axis2,[5] and
Apache Tomcat. In our prototype design, WSRec controls a number of distributed
computers in different countries from PlanetLab[6] for monitoring the publicly
available real-world Web services and collecting their QoS performance data.
These collected real-world Web service QoS data are employed for studying the
performance of our prediction approach. Figure 4.2 shows the architecture of
WSRec, which includes the following components:

- The *Input Handler* receives and processes the Web service QoS values provided
  by an active service user.
- The *Find Similar Users* module finds similar users from the training users of
  WSRec for the active user.
- The *Predict Missing Data* module predicts the missing QoS values for the active
  user using our approach and saves the predicted values.
- The *Recommender* module employs the predicted QoS values to recommend
  optimal Web services to the active user. This module also returns all predicted
  values to the active user.

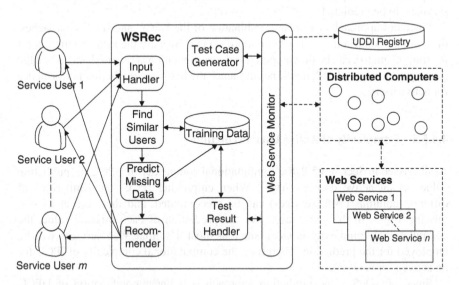

Fig. 4.2 Architecture of WSRec

---

[5]http://ws.apache.org/axis2
[6]http://www.planet-lab.org

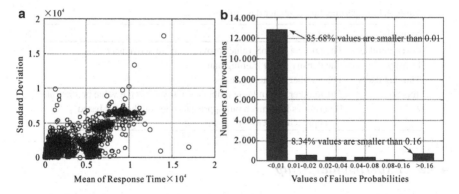

Fig. 4.3 Value distribution of user-item matrix

- The *Test Case Generator* generates test cases for the Web service evaluations. Axis2 is employed for generating test cases automatically in our implementation.
- The *Training Data* stores the collected Web service QoS values, which will be employed for predicting missing values of the active user. The *Test Result Handler* collects the Web service evaluation results from the distributed computers.
- The *Web Service Monitor* controls a set of distributed computers to monitor the Web services and record their QoS performance.

We randomly selected 100 Web services which are located in 22 countries for our experiments. Some of the initially selected Web services had to be replaced due to (1) authentication required, (2) permanent invocation failure (e.g., the Web service is shutdown), and (3) too long processing duration. 150 computers in 24 countries from PlanetLab [2] were employed to monitor and collect QoS information on the selected Web services. About 1.5 million Web service invocations were executed and the test results were collected.

By processing the experimental results, we obtained a 150 × 100 user-item matrix, where each entry in the matrix is a vector including two QoS values, that is, *response time* and *failure probability*. *Response time* represents the time duration between the client sending a request and receiving a response, while *failure probability* represents the ratio between the number of invocation failures and the total number of invocations. In our experiments, each service user invokes each Web service 100 times. Figures 4.3a, b show the value distributions of *response time* and *failure probability* of the 15,000 entries in the matrix, respectively. Figure 4.3a shows that the means of response times of most entries were smaller than 5,000 milliseconds and different Web service invocations contained large variances in the real environment. Figure 4.3b shows that failure probabilities of most entries (85.68%) were smaller than 1%, while failure probabilities of a small number of entries (8.34%) were larger than 16%. In the following sections, the unit of response time is milliseconds.

Table 4.1 Experimental parameter descriptions

Symbols	Descriptions
Given number	The number of QoS values provided by an active user
Density	The density of the training matrix
Training users	The number of training users
Top-K	The number of similar neighbors employed for the value prediction
λ	Determines how much our approach relies on the user-based approach or item-based approach

4.5.2 Experimental Setup

We divided the 150 service users into two parts, one part as training users and the other part as active users. For the training matrix, we randomly removed entries to make the matrix sparser with different density (e.g., 10%, 20%). For an active user, we also randomly removed a different number of entries and named the number of remaining entries as *given number*, which denotes the number of entries (QoS values) provided by the active user. Different methods were employed for predicting the QoS values of the removed entries. The original values of the removed entries were used as the expected values to study the prediction accuracy. The experimental parameters and their descriptions are summarized in Table 4.1.

We used mean absolute error (MAE) and root mean square error (RMSE) metrics to measure the prediction quality of our method in comparison with other collaborative filtering methods. MAE is defined as

$$\text{MAE} = \frac{\sum_{i,j} \left| r_{i,j} - \hat{r}_{i,j} \right|}{N}, \tag{4.17}$$

and RMSE is defined as

$$\text{RMSE} = \sqrt{\frac{\sum_{i,j} \left(r_{i,j} - \hat{r}_{i,j} \right)^2}{N}}, \tag{4.18}$$

where $r_{i,j}$ denotes the expected QoS value of Web service j observed by user i, $\hat{r}_{i,j}$ is the predicted QoS value, and N is the number of predicted values.

4.5.3 Performance Comparison

To study the prediction performance, we compared our approach (named as WSRec) with four other well-known approaches: user mean (UMEAN), item mean (IMEAN), user-based prediction algorithm using PCC (UPCC) [1], and item-based algorithm using PCC (IPCC) [9]. UMEAN employs the average QoS performance

Table 4.2 MAE and RMSE comparison with basic approaches (a smaller MAE or RMSE value means a better performance)

| Metric | Density (%) | Methods | Training users = 100 | | | | | |
| | | | Response time | | | Failure probability | | |
			G10	G20	G30	G10 (%)	G20 (%)	G30 (%)
MAE	**10**	UMEAN	1,623	1,539	1,513	5.71	5.58	5.53
		IMEAN	903	901	907	2.40	2.36	2.46
		UPCC	1,148	877	810	4.85	4.20	3.86
		IPCC	768	736	736	2.24	2.16	2.21
		WSRec	**758**	**700**	**672**	**2.21**	**2.08**	**2.08**
	20	UMEAN	1,585	1,548	1,508	5.74	5.53	5.51
		IMEAN	866	859	861	2.36	2.34	2.29
		UPCC	904	722	626	4.40	3.43	2.85
		IPCC	606	610	639	2.01	1.98	1.98
		WSRec	**586**	**551**	**546**	**1.93**	**1.80**	**1.70**
	30	UMEAN	1,603	1,543	1,508	5.64	5.58	5.56
		IMEAN	856	854	853	2.26	2.29	2.30
		UPCC	915	671	572	4.25	3.25	2.58
		IPCC	563	566	602	1.84	1.83	1.86
		WSRec	**538**	**504**	**499**	**1.78**	**1.69**	**1.63**
RMSE	**10**	UMEAN	3,339	3,250	3,192	15.47	15.04	14.74
		IMEAN	1,441	1,436	1,442	5.61	5.58	5.85
		UPCC	2,036	1,455	1,335	10.84	7.51	6.55
		IPCC	1,335	1,288	1,278	5.36	5.27	5.53
		WSRec	**1,329**	**1,247**	**1,197**	**5.31**	**5.12**	**5.11**
	20	UMEAN	3,332	3,240	3,211	15.49	15.05	14.80
		IMEAN	1,269	1,252	1,257	4.67	4.62	4.54
		UPCC	1,356	1,128	1,019	8.07	5.31	4.58
		IPCC	1,020	1,016	1,056	4.15	4.13	4.12
		WSRec	**997**	**946**	**937**	**4.04**	**3.83**	**3.67**
	30	UMEAN	3,336	3,246	3,197	15.49	15.00	14.68
		IMEAN	1,207	1,209	1,203	4.21	4.23	4.22
		UPCC	1,267	1,035	924	7.72	5.09	4.15
		IPCC	950	957	995	3.72	3.71	3.75
		WSRec	**921**	**884**	**869**	**3.64**	**3.46**	**3.37**

of the current service user on other Web services to predict the QoS performance of other Web services, while IMEAN employs the average QoS performance of the Web service observed by other service users to predict the QoS performance for the current active user. UPCC only employs similar users for the QoS performance prediction by employing Eq. (4.7), while IPCC only employs similar Web services for the prediction by employing Eq. (4.8).

Table 4.2 shows the MAE and RMSE results of different prediction methods on *response time* and *failure probability* employing 10, 20, and 30% densities of the training matrix, respectively. For the active users, we varied the number of provided QoS values (*given number*) as 10, 20, and 30 by randomly removing entries (named as G10, G20, and G30, respectively, in Table 4.2). We set the number of training users to 100 and set $\lambda = 0.1$, since the item-based approach achieves better prediction accuracy than the user-based approach in our Web service QoS dataset. The detailed investigation of the λ value setting will be shown in Sect. 4.5.8. Each experiment was run 50 times and the average MAE and RMSE values are reported. We did not report the confidence interval of the experiments since those values are very small.

The experimental results of Table 4.2 show that:

- Under all experimental settings, our WSRec method obtains smaller MAE and RMSE values consistently, which indicates better prediction accuracy.
- The MAE and RMSE values of WSRec become smaller with the increase in the given number from 10 to 30, indicating that the prediction accuracy can be improved by providing more QoS values.
- When increasing the training matrix density from 10 to 30%, the prediction accuracy is also enhanced significantly, since a denser training matrix provides more information for the prediction.

The item-based approaches (IMEAN, IPCC) outperform the user-based approaches (UMEAN, UPCC). This observation indicates that similar Web services provide more information than similar users for the prediction in our user-item matrix.

4.5.4 Impact of the Missing Value Prediction

The *missing value prediction* in Sect. 4.4.2 makes use of the similar users and similar items to predict the missing values of the training matrix to make it denser. Our WSRec method alleviates the potential negative influences of bad prediction on the missing data by not predicting the missing value if it has neither similar users nor similar items. To study the impact of the *missing value prediction*, we implemented two versions of WSRec. One version employs missing value prediction while the other version does not. In the experiments, we varied the *given number* of the active users from 5 to 50 with a step value of 5 and varied the values of *training users* from 20 to 140 with a step value of 20. In reality, the training matrix is usually very sparse. Therefore, we set the *density* = 10% to make the training matrix sparser. We also set *Top-K* = 10, which means that the top 10 similar neighbors will be employed for value prediction.

Figure 4.4 shows the experimental results, where Figs. 4.4a–d show the experimental results of *response time* and Figs. 4.4e–h show the experimental results of *failure probability*. Figure 4.4 indicates that:

- *WSRec with missing value prediction* outperforms *WSRec without missing value prediction* consistently in all experimental settings, indicating that by predicting missing values for the training matrix, we are able to obtain more accurate prediction results.

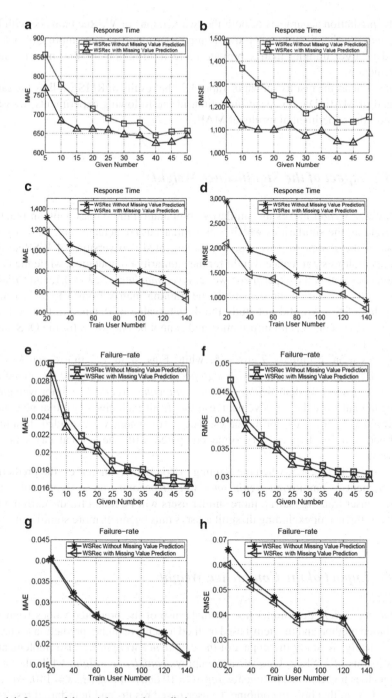

Fig. 4.4 Impact of the training matrix prediction

- The prediction accuracies of both the two versions of WSRec enhance with the increase in the given number and training user number, since more QoS values and a larger training matrix provide more information for the missing value prediction.
- The same as the results shown in Table 4.2, the results of RMSE follow the same trend of MAE. Due to space limitation, in the following experiments, we only report the experimental results of MAE.

4.5.5 Impact of the Significance Weight

Significance weight makes the similarity computation more reasonable in practice by devaluing the similarities which look similar but are actually not. To study the impact of the *significance weight*, we implemented two versions of WSRec: one version employs significance weight for the similarity computation, while the other version does not. In the experiment, we set *given number* $= 5$, $\lambda = 0.1$, and *training users* $= 140$. We varied the density of the training matrix from 5 to 50% with a step value of 5%. We did not study the density value of 0, since in that case the training matrix contains no information and cannot be employed for the QoS value prediction.

Figures 4.5a, c employ *Top-K* $= 5$, while Figs. 4.5b, d employ *Top-K* $= 10$. Figure 4.5 shows that *WSRec with significance weight* obtains better prediction accuracy consistently than *WSRec without significance weight*. The improvement is not significant since the improvement resulting from excluding dissimilar neighbors is alleviated in a lot of normal cases. The cases where we excluded dissimilar neighbors did not happen very often compared with the normal cases in our experiments.

As shown in Fig. 4.5, when the training matrix density increases, the prediction improvement of employing *significance weight* becomes more significant, since with a denser training matrix, more similar users will be found for the current user and the influence of excluding dissimilar users thus becomes more significant.

4.5.6 Impact of the Confidence Weight

Confidence weight determines how to make use of the predicted values from the user-based method and the item-based method to achieve higher prediction accuracy automatically. To study the impact of the *confidence weight*, we also implemented two versions of WSRec. One version employs *confidence weight*, while the other version does not. In the experiments, *Top-K* $= 10$ and *training users* $= 140$. We also set $\lambda = 0.5$, so that how to combine the user-based results and item-based results is not influenced by λ and is determined by the confidence weight alone.

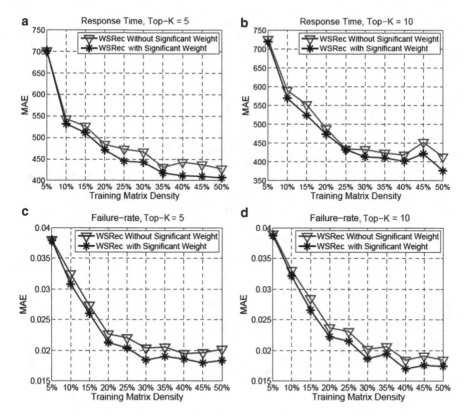

Fig. 4.5 Impact of significance weight

Figures 4.6a, c show the experimental results with given number change, while Fig. 4.6b, d show the experimental results with training matrix density change. As shown in Fig. 4.6, *WSRec with confidence weight* outperforms *WSRec without confidence weight* for both the *response time* and *failure probability*. Figure 4.6 also shows that the MAE values become smaller with the increase in the given number and the training matrix density, which is consistent with the observation from Table 4.2.

4.5.7   Impact of Enhanced Top-K

In our *WSRec* prediction method, we exclude dissimilar users with negative PCC values from the Top-K similar neighbors by using an enhanced Top-K algorithm. To study the impact of our enhanced Top-K algorithm on the prediction results, we implemented two versions of *WSRec*. One version employs enhanced Top-K, while the other does not. Figures 4.7a, c show the experimental results of response

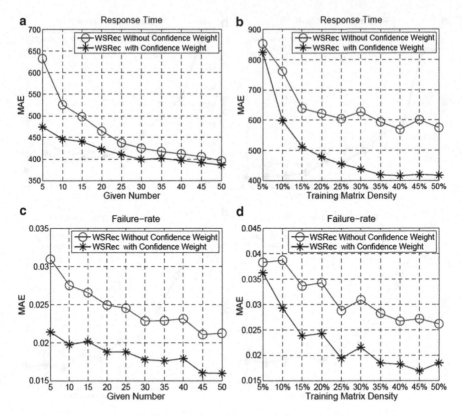

Fig. 4.6 Impact of confidence weight

time and failure probability with given number change in the experimental settings of *density* = 10%, *training users* = 140, $\lambda = 0.1$, and *Top-K* = 10. Figures 4.7b, d shows the MAE values with *Top-K* value change in the experimental settings of *density* = 10%, *given number* = 5, and *training users* = 140.

Figure 4.7 shows that *WSRec with the enhanced Top-K* outperforms *WSRec without the enhanced Top-K* for both the *response time* and *failure probability*. The prediction performance of *WSRec without the enhanced Top-K* is not stable, since it may include dissimilar neighbors, which will greatly influence the prediction accuracy. Moreover, as shown in Figs. 4.7a, c, while the given number increases, differences in the two WSRec versions in MAE decrease. Since with a larger given number, more similar users can be found for the current active user, the probability of selecting dissimilar users with negative PCC values as the top 10 similar users (*Top-K* = 10 in the experiment) is small. Our enhanced Top-K algorithm works only in situations where the number of similar users is smaller than the value of Top-K. Figure 4.7 shows that the parameter Top-K can be set to be a large value for obtaining optimal performance in our WSRec approach.

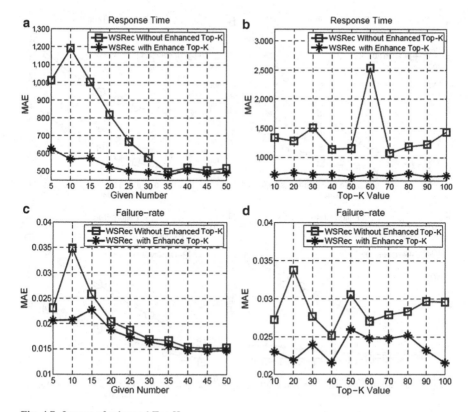

Fig. 4.7 Impact of enhanced Top-K

4.5.8   Impact of λ

Different datasets may have different data correlation characteristics. Parameter λ makes our prediction method more feasible and adaptable to different datasets. If $\lambda = 1$, we only extract information from the similar users, and if $\lambda = 0$, we only consider valuable information from the similar items. In other cases, we fuse information from both similar users and similar items based on the value of λ to predict the missing value for active users.

To study the impact of the parameter λ on our collaborative filtering method, we set *Top-K* = 10 and *training users* = 140. We varied the value of λ from 0 to 1 with a step value of 0.1. Figures 4.8a, c show the results of *given number* = 10, *given number* = 20, and *given number* = 30 with 20% density training matrix of *response time* and *failure probability*, respectively. Figures 4.8b, d show the results of *density* = 10%, *density* = 20%, and *density* = 30% with *given number* = 20 of *response time* and *failure probability*, respectively.

Observing Fig. 4.8, we drew the conclusion that the value of λ impacts the recommendation results significantly, and a suitable λ value will provide better

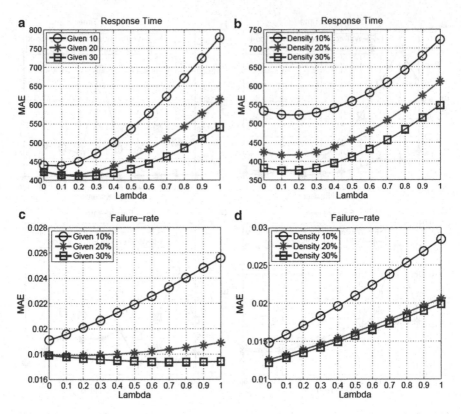

Fig. 4.8 Impact of λ

prediction accuracy. Another interesting observation is that, in Fig. 4.8a, with the given number increasing from 10 to 30, the optimal value of λ, which obtains the minimal MAE values of the curves in the figure, shifts from 0.1 to 0.3. This indicates that the optimal λ value is influenced by the given number. Similar to the observation in Figs. 4.8a, c the optimal value of λ for *failure probability* shifts from 0 to 0.7, indicating that the optimal λ value is influenced not only by the given number but also by the nature of the datasets. For both the *response time* and *failure probability*, the similar items are more important than the similar users when limited Web service QoS values are given by the active users, while the similar users become more important when more QoS values are available from the active users. This observation is also confirmed by the experimental results reported in Table 4.2, where the IPCC outperforms the UPCC for all the *given number* = 10, *given number* = 20, and *given number* = 30. This is reasonable, since with limited user-given QoS values, the UMEAN prediction method, which employs the mean of the user-given QoS values to predict the QoS values of other Web services for this user, exhibits a higher probability of being inaccurate. This will influence the prediction performance of UPCC, which is based on the value predicted by UMEAN for the missing value prediction as shown in Eq. (4.7).

As shown in Figs. 4.8b, d, with the given number of 20 all the three curves (*density* 10, 20, *and* 30%) of *response time* and *failure probability* obtain the best prediction performance with the same λ value ($\lambda = 0.2$ for *response time* and $\lambda = 0$ for *failure probability*), indicating that the optimal λ value is not influenced by the training matrix density.

4.6 Summary

In this chapter, we propose a neighborhood-based approach for predicting QoS values of Web services by systematically combining the user-based PCC approach and the item-based PCC approach. Large-scale real-world experiments are conducted, and the comprehensive experimental results show the effectiveness and feasibility of our approach.

Our ongoing research includes collecting QoS performance of more real-world Web services from more service users. More investigations will be conducted for QoS value updates, since the QoS values of Web services are changing from time to time in reality. In our Web service evaluations reported in this chapter, to reduce the effect of the Web service invocations on the real-world Web services, we only selected one operation from a Web service for making evaluations and employed the performance of this operation to present the performance of the Web service. More investigations will be conducted on different operations of the same Web service in our future work.

References

1. Breese JS, Heckerman D, Kadie C (1998) Empirical analysis of predictive algorithms for collaborative filtering. In: Proceedings of the 14th annual conference on uncertainty in artificial intelligence (UAI'98). Morgan Kaufmann Publishers, San Francisco, pp 43–52
2. Chun B, Culler D, Roscoe T, Bavier A, Peterson L, Wawrzoniak M, Bowman M (2003) Planetlab: an overlay testbed for broad-coverage services. ACM SIGCOMM Comput Commun Rev 33(3):3–12
3. Deora V, Shao J, Gray W, Fiddian N (2003) A quality of service management framework based on user expectations. In: Proceedings of the 1st international conference on service-oriented computing (ICSOC'03), Trento, Italy, pp 104–114
4. Deshpande M, Karypis G (2004) Item-based top-n recommendation. ACM Trans Inf Syst 22(1):143–177
5. Herlocker JL, Konstan JA, Borchers A, Riedl J (1999) An algorithmic framework for performing collaborative filtering. In: Proceedings of the 22nd international ACM SIGIR conference on research and development in information retrieval (SIGIR'99), Berkeley, CA, USA, pp 230–237
6. Jin R, Chai JY, Si L (2004) An automatic weighting scheme for collaborative filtering. In: Proceedings of the 27th international ACM SIGIR conference on research and development in information retrieval (SIGIR'04), Sheffield, UK, pp 337–344
7. Linden G, Smith B, York J (2003) Amazon.com recommendations: item-to-item collaborative filtering. IEEE Internet Comput 7(1):76–80

8. McLaughlin MR, Herlocker JL (2004) A collaborative filtering algorithm and evaluation metric that accurately model the user experience. In: Proceedings of the 27th international ACM SIGIR conference on research and development in information retrieval (SIGIR'04), Sheffield, UK, pp 329–336
9. Sarwar B, Karypis G, Konstan J, Riedl J (2001) Item-based collaborative filtering recommendation algorithms. In: Proceedings of the 10th international conference on World Wide Web (WWW'01). ACM Press, New York, pp 285–295
10. Su X, Khoshgoftaar TM, Zhu X, Greiner R (2008) Imputation-boosted collaborative filtering using machine learning classifiers. In: Proceedings of the ACM symposium on applied computing (SAC'08). ACM Press, New York, pp 949–950
11. Wu G, Wei J, Qiao X, Li L (2007) A Bayesian network based QoS assessment model for Web services. In: Proceedings of the international conference on services computing (SCC'07), Salt Lake City, UT, pp 498–505
12. Xue G, Lin C, Yang Q, Xi W, Zeng H, Yu Y, Chen Z (2005) Scalable collaborative filtering using cluster-based smoothing. In: Proceedings of the 28th international ACM SIGIR conference on research and development in information retrieval (SIGIR'05), Salvador, Brazil, pp 114–121
13. Yu T, Zhang Y, Lin KJ (2007) Efficient algorithms for Web services selection with end-to-end QoS constraints. ACM Trans Web 1(1):1–26
14. Zeng L, Benatallah B, Ngu AH, Dumas M, Kalagnanam J, Chang H (2004) QoS-aware middleware for Web services composition. IEEE Trans Softw Eng 30(5):311–327
15. Zheng Z, Lyu MR (2008) A distributed replication strategy evaluation and selection framework for fault-tolerant Web services. In: Proceedings of the 6th international conference on Web services (ICWS'08), Beijing, China, pp 145–152
16. Zheng Z, Lyu MR (2009) A QoS-aware fault tolerant middleware for dependable service composition. In: Proceedings of the 39th international conference on dependable systems and networks (DSN'09), Lisbon, Portugal, pp 239–248
17. Zheng Z, Ma H, Lyu MR, King I (2009) WSRec: a collaborative filtering based Web service recommender system. In: Proceedings of the 7th international conference on Web services (ICWS'09), Los Angeles, CA, pp 437–444

Chapter 5
Model-Based QoS Prediction of Web Services

Abstract The neighborhood-based QoS prediction approach has several drawbacks, including (1) the computation complexity is too high and (2) it is not easy to find similar users/items when the user-item matrix is very sparse. To address these drawbacks, this chapter proposes a neighborhood-integrated matrix factorization (NIMF) approach for Web service QoS value prediction. Our approach explores the social wisdom of service users by systematically fusing the neighborhood-based and the model-based collaborative filtering approaches to achieve higher prediction accuracy.

Keywords Model-based prediction • Matrix factorization • QoS prediction

5.1 Overview

The neighborhood-based QoS prediction approach [6, 15, 16] has several drawbacks, including (1) the computational complexity is too high and (2) it is not easy to find similar users/items when the user-item matrix is very sparse. To address these drawbacks, we propose a neighborhood-integrated matrix factorization (NIMF) approach for Web service QoS value prediction in this chapter. The idea is that client-side Web service QoS values of a service user can be predicted by taking advantage of the social wisdom of service users, that is, the past Web service usage experiences of other service users. By the collaboration of different service users, the QoS values of a Web service can be effectively predicted in our approach even if the current user did not conduct any evaluation of the Web service and has no idea of its internal design and implementation details.

In this chapter, firstly we propose a neighborhood-integrated matrix factorization (NIMF) approach for personalized Web service QoS value prediction.

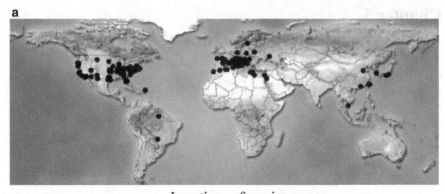

Locations of service users

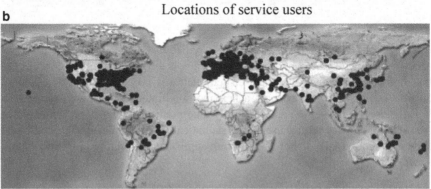

Locations of Web services

Fig. 5.1 Location information: (**a**) Locations of service users, totally 339 service users from 30 countries are plotted; (**b**) Locations of Web services; in total 5,825 real-world Web services from 73 countries are plotted. Each user in (**a**) invoked all Web services in (**b**). Totally 1,974,675 Web service invocation results were collected

Our approach explores the social wisdom of service users by systematically fusing the neighborhood-based [1, 2, 5, 12] and the model-based collaborative filtering approaches [7, 8, 10, 11] to achieve higher prediction accuracy compared with the neighborhood-based prediction approach. Secondly, we conduct large-scale experiments and release a real-world Web service QoS dataset for future research. To the best of our knowledge, the scale of our released Web service QoS dataset (including 339 distributed service users and 5,825 real-world Web services as shown in Fig. 5.1) is the largest in the field of service computing. Based on this dataset, extensive experimental investigations are conducted to study the QoS value prediction accuracy of our approach.

The rest of this chapter is organized as follows: Sect. 5.2 presents our QoS value prediction approach. Section 5.3 describes our experiments, and Sect. 5.4 concludes this chapter.

5.2 Model-Based QoS Prediction

Based on the collected Web service QoS values from different service users, in this section, we first describe the Web service QoS value prediction problem in Sect. 5.2.1, and then propose a solution in Sects. 5.2.2, 5.2.3, and 5.2.4.

5.2.1 Problem Description

The process of Web service QoS value prediction usually includes a user-item matrix as shown in Fig. 5.2a, where each entry in this matrix represents the value of a certain QoS property (e.g., *response time* in this example) of a Web service (e.g., i_1 to i_6) observed by a service user (e.g., u_1 to u_5). As shown in Fig. 5.2a, each service user has several response-time values of their invoked Web services. Similarities between two different users in the matrix can be calculated by analyzing their QoS values of the same Web services. The Pearson Correlation Coefficient (PCC) [9] is usually employed for the similarity computation. As shown in the similarity graph in Fig. 5.2b, in total five users (nodes u_1 to u_5) are connected with ten edges. Each edge is associated with a PCC value in the range of $[-1, 1]$ to specify the similarity between user u_i and user u_j, where a larger PCC value stands for higher similarity.

a	i_1	i_2	i_3	i_4	i_5	i_6
u_1	0.5	1.2		0.3		0.4
u_2		0.8		0.6	0.5	
u_3	0.4		0.3		0.9	
u_4		0.6		0.7		
u_5	0.5		0.7			0.3

b

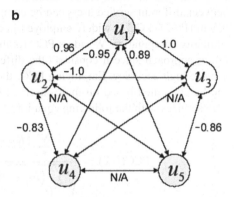

Fig. 5.2 A toy example (**a**) User-item matrix (**b**) User similarities

The symbol *N/A* means that the similarity between user u_i and user u_j is non-available, since they do not have any commonly invoked Web services. The problem we study in this chapter is how to accurately predict the missing QoS values in the user-item matrix by employing the available QoS values. By predicting the Web service QoS values in the user-item matrix, we can provide personalized QoS value prediction of the unused Web services for the service users, who can employ these Web service QoS values for making service selection, service ranking, automatic service composition, etc.

To obtain the missing values in the user-item matrix, we can employ the Web service QoS values observed by other service users for predicting the Web service performance for the current user. However, since service users are in different geographic locations and are under different network conditions, the current user may not be able to experience similar QoS performance as other service users. To address this challenging Web service QoS value prediction problem, we propose a neighborhood-integrated matrix factorization (NIMF) approach, which makes the best utilization of both the local information of similar users and the global information of all the available QoS values in the user-item matrix to achieve better prediction accuracy. Our approach is designed as a two-phase process. In phase 1, we calculate the user similarities using PCC and determine a set of Top-K similar users for the current user. Then, based on the neighborhood information, we propose a neighborhood-integrated matrix factorization approach to predict the missing values in the user-item matrix in phase 2. Details of these two phases are presented in Sects. 5.2.2 and 5.2.3, respectively.

5.2.2 Neighborhood Similarity Computation

Given an $m \times n$ user-item matrix R consists of m service users and n Web services, each entry in this matrix R_{ij} represents the value of a certain client-side QoS property of Web service j observed by service user i. If user i did not invoke the Web service j before, then $R_{ij} = $ null. Employing the available Web service QoS values in the user-item matrix, which are collected from different service users, the similarities between different service users can be computed by the Pearson Correlation Coefficient (PCC). PCC is widely employed in a number of recommender systems for similarity computation. We adopt PCC for the neighborhood similarity computation in our approach since it considers the differences in the user value style and can achieve high accuracy. Employing PCC, the similarity between two users i and k can be computed based on their observed QoS values of the commonly invoked Web services with the following equation:

$$
\mathrm{PCC}(i,k) = \frac{\sum\limits_{j \in J} \left(R_{ij} - \overline{R}_i \right) \left(R_{kj} - \overline{R}_k \right)}{\sqrt{\sum\limits_{j \in J} \left(R_{ij} - \overline{R}_i \right)^2} \sqrt{\sum\limits_{j \in J} \left(R_{kj} - \overline{R}_k \right)^2}}, \tag{5.1}
$$

where j is the subset of Web services which are invoked by both user i and user k, R_{ij} is the QoS value of Web service j observed by service user i, and $\overline{R}_i$ and $\overline{R}_k$ are the average QoS values of different Web services observed by service user i and k, respectively. From this definition, the similarity of two service users i and k, PCC (i, k), is in the interval of $[-1, 1]$, where a larger PCC value indicates higher user similarity.

After calculating the similarities between the current user and other users, a set of Top-K similar users can be identified based on the PCC values. In practice, a service user may have a limited number of similar users. Traditional Top-K algorithms ignore this problem and still include dissimilar users with negative PCC values, which will greatly influence the prediction accuracy. In our approach, we exclude the dissimilar service users who have negative correlations (negative PCC values). For a service user i, a set of similar users $T(i)$ can be therefore identified by the following equation:

$$T(i) = \{k | k \in \text{Top-K}(i), \text{PCC}(i, k) > 0, i \neq k\}, \tag{5.2}$$

where Top-K (i) is a set of the Top-K similar users to the current user i and PCC(i, k) is the PCC similarity value between user i and user k, which can be calculated by Eq. (5.1). Note that the Top-K relations are not symmetrical. That user k is among the Top-K neighbors of user i does not necessary indicate that user i is also among the Top-K neighbors of user k. With the neighborhood information, we can now design our neighborhood-integrated matrix factorization model for the QoS value prediction.

5.2.3 Neighborhood-Integrated Matrix Factorization

A popular approach to predict missing values is to fit a factor model to the user-item matrix, and use this factor model to make further predictions. The premise behind a low-dimensional factor model is that there are a small number of factors influencing the QoS usage experiences, and that a user's QoS usage experience on a Web service is determined by how each factor applies to the user and the Web service.

Consider an $m \times n$ user-item matrix R. The matrix factorization method employs a rank-l matrix $X = U^T V$ to fit it, where $U \in R^{l \times m}$ and $V \in R^{l \times n}$. From the above definition, we can see that the low-dimensional matrices U and V are unknown, and need to be estimated. Moreover, this feature representation has clear physical meanings. In this linear factor model, a user's Web service QoS values correspond to a linear combination of the factor vectors, with user-specific coefficients. More specifically, each column of U performs as a "feature vector" for a user, and each column of V is a linear predictor for a Web service, predicting the entries in the corresponding column of the user-item matrix R based on the "features" in U.

By adding the constraints of the norms of U and V to penalize large values of U and V, we have the following optimization problem [10]:

$$\min_{U,V} L(R, U, V) = \frac{1}{2} \sum_{i=1}^{m} \sum_{j=1}^{n} I_{ij}^{R} \left(R_{ij} - U_i^T V_j \right)^2 + \frac{\lambda_U}{2} \|U\|_F^2 + \frac{\lambda_V}{2} \|V\|_F^2,$$

(5.3)

where I_{ij}^{R} is the indicator function that is equal to 1 if the user u_i invoked Web service v_j and equal to 0 otherwise. $\|.\|_F^2$ denotes the Frobenius norm, and λ_U and λ_V are the two parameters. The optimization problem in Eq. (5.3) minimizes the sum-of-squared-errors objective function with quadratic regularization terms. It also has a probabilistic interpretation with Gaussian observation noise, which is detailed in [10].

The above approach utilizes the global information of all the available QoS values in the user-item matrix for predicting missing values. This approach is generally effective at estimating overall structure (global information) that relates simultaneously to all users or items. However, this model is poor at detecting strong associations among a small set of closely related users or items (local information), precisely where the neighborhood models would perform better. Normally, the available Web service QoS values in the user-item matrix are very sparse; hence, neither the matrix factorization nor neighborhood-based approaches can generate optimal QoS values. In order to preserve both global information and local information mentioned above, we employ a balance parameter to fuse these two types of information. The idea is that every time when factorizing a QoS value, we treat it as the ensemble of a user's information and the user's neighbors' information. The neighbors of the current user can be obtained by employing Eq. (5.2). Hence, we can minimize the following sum-of-squared-errors objective functions with quadratic regularization terms:

$$L(R, S, U, V) = \frac{1}{2} \sum_{i=1}^{m} \sum_{j=1}^{n} I_{ij}^{R} \left(R_{ij} - \left(\alpha U_i^T V_j + (1 - \alpha) \sum_{k \in T(i)} S_{ik} U_k^T V_j \right) \right)^2$$

$$+ \frac{\lambda_U}{2} \|U\|_F^2 + \frac{\lambda_V}{2} \|V\|_F^2,$$

(5.4)

where $T(i)$ is a set of Top-K similar users of user u_i and S_{ik} is the normalized similarity score between user u_i and user u_k, which can be calculated by

$$S_{ik} = \frac{PCC(i, k)}{\sum_{k \in T(i)} PCC(i, k)}.$$

(5.5)

A local minimum of the objective function given by Eq. (5.4) can be found by performing a gradient descent in U_i, V_j,

$$\frac{\partial L}{\partial U_i} = \alpha \sum_{j=1}^{n} I_{ij}^R V_j \left(\left(\alpha U_i^T V_j + (1-\alpha) \sum_{k \in T(i)} S_{ik} U_k^T V_j \right) - R_{ij} \right)$$

$$+ (1-\alpha) \sum_{p \in B(i)} \sum_{j=1}^{n} I_{pj}^R S_{pi} V_j \left(\left(\alpha U_p^T V_j + (1-\alpha) \sum_{k \in T(p)} S_{pk} U_k^T V_j \right) - R_{pj} \right) + \lambda_U U_i,$$

$$\frac{\partial L}{\partial V_j} = \sum_{i=1}^{m} I_{ij}^R \left(\left(\alpha U_i^T V_j + (1-\alpha) \sum_{k \in T(i)} S_{ik} U_k^T V_j \right) - R_{ij} \right)$$

$$\times \left(\alpha U_i + (1-\alpha) \sum_{k \in T(i)} S_{ik} U_k^T \right) + \lambda_V V_j, \tag{5.6}$$

where $B(i)$ is the set that includes all the users who are the neighbors of user u_i. In order to reduce the model complexity, in all of the experiments we conduct, we set $\lambda_U = \lambda_V$.

5.2.4 Complexity Analysis

The main computation of the gradient methods is to evaluate the object function L and its gradients against the variables. Because of the sparsity of matrices R and S, the computational complexity of evaluating the object function L is $O(\rho_R l + \rho_R K l)$, where ρ_R is the number of nonzero entries in the matrix R, and K is the number of similar neighbors. K is normally a small number since a large number of K will introduce noise, which will potentially hurt the prediction accuracy. The computational complexities for the gradients $\frac{\partial L}{\partial U}$ and $\frac{\partial L}{\partial V}$ in Eq. (5.6) are $O(\rho_R K l + \rho_R K^2 l)$ and $O(\rho_R l + \rho_R K l)$, respectively. Therefore, the total computational complexity in one iteration is $O(\rho_R K l + \rho_R K^2 l)$ which indicates that, theoretically, the computational time of our method is linear with respect to the number of observations in the user-item matrix R. This complexity analysis shows that our proposed approach is very efficient and can scale to very large datasets.

5.3 Experiments

In this section, we conduct experiments to compare the prediction accuracy of our NIMF approach with other state-of-the-art collaborative filtering methods. Our experiments are intended to address the following questions: (1) How does

Table 5.1 Statistics of the
WS QoS dataset

Statistics	Values
Num. of service users	339
Num. of Web services	5,825
Num. of Web service invocations	1,974,675
Range of response time	1–20 s
Range of throughput	1–1,000 kbps

our approach compare with the published state-of-the-art collaborative filtering
algorithms? (2) How does the model parameter α affect the prediction accuracy?
(3) What is the impact of the *matrix density, Top-K values*, and *dimensionality* on
the prediction accuracy?

5.3.1   Dataset Description

We implement a *WSCrawler* and a *WSEvaluator* employing JDK 6.0, Eclipse 3.3,
and Axis2.[1] Employing our *WSCrawler*, addresses of 5,825 openly accessible Web
services are obtained by crawling Web service information from www.seekda.com,
a well-known Web service search engine. Axis2 is employed to generate client-side
Web service invocation codes and test cases automatically. In total, 78,635 Java
classes and 13,644,507 lines of Java codes are generated in our experiments.

To evaluate the QoS performance of real-world Web services from distributed
locations, we deployed our *WSEvaluator* to 339 distributed computers of Planet-
Lab,[2] which is a distributed test-bed made up of computers all over the world. In
our experiment, each PlanetLab computer invokes all the Web services. As shown
in Fig. 5.1, in total 1,974,675 real-world Web service invocation results are collected
from these 339 service users on 5,825 real-world Web services. The scale of our real-
world Web service evaluation is the largest among the published works on service
computing as far as we know.

By processing the invocation results, we obtained two $339 \times 5,825$ user-item
matrices. One matrix contains response-time values, while the other one contains
throughput values. The statistics of our Web service QoS dataset is summarized in
Table 5.1, the distributions of response-time and throughput values are shown in
Fig. 5.3, and more experimental details (e.g., detailed lists of service users and Web
services, the user-item matrix, the detailed Web service invocation results) were
released online[3] for future research. As shown in Table 5.1, the ranges of response
time and throughput are 0–20 and 0–1,000 kbps (*kilobits per second*), respectively.
Figure 5.3a shows that 91% of the response-time values are smaller than 2 s, and
Fig. 5.3b shows that 89.5% of the throughput values are smaller than 100 kbps.

---

[1]http://ws.apache.org/axis2

[2]http://www.planet-lab.org

[3]http://www.wsdream.net

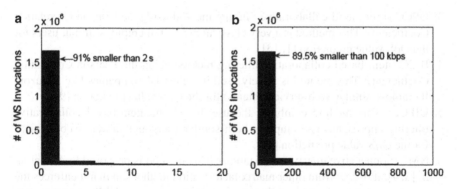

Fig. 5.3 Value distribution (**a**) Values of response-time (**b**) Values of throughput

5.3.2   Metrics

We use mean absolute error (MAE) and root mean square error (RMSE) metrics to measure the prediction quality of our method in comparison with other collaborative filtering methods. MAE is defined as

$$\text{MAE} = \frac{\sum_{i,j} |R_{ij} - \hat{R}_{ij}|}{N}, \tag{5.7}$$

and RMSE is defined as

$$\text{RMSE} = \sqrt{\frac{\sum_{i,j} \left(R_{ij} - \hat{R}_{ij}\right)^2}{N}}, \tag{5.8}$$

where R_{ij} denotes the expected QoS value of Web service j observed by user i, $\hat{R}_{ij}$ is the predicted QoS value, and N is the number of predicted values.

5.3.3   Comparison

In this section, in order to show the prediction accuracy of our NIMF approach, we compared our method with the following approaches:

1. UMEAN (user mean): This method employs a service user's average QoS value on the used Web services to predict the QoS values of the unused Web services.
2. IMEAN (item mean): This method employs the average QoS value of the Web service observed by other service users to predict the QoS value for a service user who never invoked this Web service previously.

3. UPCC (user-based collaborative filtering method using the Pearson Correlation Coefficient): This method is a very classical method. It employs similar users for the QoS value prediction [1, 13].
4. IPCC (item-based collaborative filtering method using the Pearson Correlation Coefficient): This method is widely used in industrial companies like Amazon. It employs similar Web services (items) for the QoS value prediction [9].
5. UIPCC: This method combines the user-based and item-based collaborative filtering approaches and employs both similar users and similar Web services for the QoS value prediction [14].
6. NMF (nonnegative matrix factorization): This method is proposed by Lee et al. in [3, 4]. It differs from other matrix factorization methods in that it enforces the constraint that the factorized factors must be nonnegative. NMF is also widely used in the collaborative filtering community.
7. PMF (probabilistic matrix factorization): This method is proposed by Salakhutdinov and Minh in [10]. It uses a user-item matrix for the recommendations, and it is based on probabilistic matrix factorization.

In the real world, the user-item matrices are usually very sparse since a service user usually only invokes a small number of Web services. In order to conduct our experiments realistically, we randomly removed entries from the user-item matrix to make the matrix sparser with different density (i.e., 5, 10, and 15%). Matrix density 5%, for example, means that we randomly selected 5% of the QoS entries to predict the remaining 95% of QoS entries. The original QoS values of the removed entries are used as the expected values to study the prediction accuracy. The above seven methods together with our NIMF method are employed for predicting the QoS values of the removed entries. The parameter settings of our NIMF method are $\alpha = 0.4$, Top-K $= 10$, $\lambda_U = \lambda_V = 0.001$, and dimensionality $= 10$ in the experiments. The experimental results are shown in Table 5.2, and the detailed investigations of parameter settings will be provided in Sects. 5.3.4, 5.3.5, 5.3.6, and 5.3.7.

From Table 5.2, we can observe that our NIMF approach obtains smaller MAE and RMSE values (indicating better prediction accuracy) consistently for both response time and throughput with different matrix densities. The MAE and RMSE values of throughput in Table 5.2 are much larger than those of the response time, since the range of throughput is 0–1,000 kbps, while the range of response time is only 0–20 s. With the increase in matrix density from 5 to 15%, the MAE and RMSE values of our NIMF method become smaller, since a denser matrix provides more information for the missing value prediction. Among all the prediction methods, our NIMF method generally achieves better performance in both MAE and RMSE, indicating that integrating the neighborhood information into a matrix factorization model can achieve higher value prediction accuracy. These experimental results demonstrate that our interpretation of the formation of QoS values is realistic and reasonable.

Table 5.2 Performance comparison

		Matrix density = 5%		Matrix density = 10%		Matrix density = 15%	
QoS	Methods	MAE	RMSE	MAE	RMSE	MAE	RMSE
Response time	UMEAN	0.8785	1.8591	0.8783	1.8555	0.8768	1.8548
(0–20 s)	IMEAN	0.7015	1.5813	0.6918	1.5440	0.6867	1.5342
	UPCC	0.6261	1.4078	0.5517	1.3151	0.5159	1.2680
	IPCC	0.6897	1.4296	0.5917	1.3268	0.5037	1.2552
	UIPCC	0.6234	1.4078	0.5365	1.3043	0.4965	1.2467
	NMF	0.6182	1.5746	0.6040	1.5494	0.5990	1.5345
	PMF	0.5678	1.4735	0.4996	1.2866	0.4720	1.2163
	NIMF	**0.5514**	**1.4075**	**0.4854**	**1.2745**	**0.4534**	**1.1980**
Throughput	UMEAN	54.0084	110.2821	53.6700	110.2977	53.8792	110.1751
(0–1,000 kbps)	IMEAN	27.3558	66.6344	26.8318	64.7674	26.6239	64.3986
	UPCC	26.1230	61.6108	21.2695	54.3701	18.7455	50.7768
	IPCC	29.2651	64.2285	27.3993	60.0825	26.4319	57.8593
	UIPCC	25.8755	60.8685	19.9754	54.8761	17.5543	47.8235
	NMF	25.7529	65.8517	17.8411	53.9896	15.8939	51.7322
	PMF	19.9034	54.0508	16.1755	46.4439	15.0956	43.7957
	NIMF	**17.9297**	**51.6573**	**16.0542**	**45.9409**	**14.4363**	**43.1596**

5.3.4 Impact of Parameter α

In our NIMF method, the parameter α controls how much our method relies on the users themselves and their similar users. If $\alpha = 1$, we only employ the users' own characteristics for making a prediction. If $\alpha = 0$, we predict the users' QoS values purely by their similar users' characteristics. In other cases, we fuse the users' own characteristics with the neighborhood information for missing QoS value prediction.

Figure 5.4 shows the impacts of parameter α on the prediction results. We observe that optimal α value settings can achieve better prediction accuracy, which demonstrates that fusing the matrix factorization methods with neighborhood-based methods will improve the prediction accuracy. No matter about response time or throughput, as α increases the MAE and RMSE values decrease (prediction accuracy increases) at first, but when α surpasses a certain threshold, the MAE and RMSE values increase (prediction accuracy decreases) with a further increase in the value of α. This phenomenon confirms the intuition that purely using the matrix factorization method or purely employing the neighborhood-based method cannot generate better QoS value prediction performance than fusing these two together.

From Figs. 5.4a, b, when using a user-item matrix with 10% density, we observe that our NIMF method achieves the best performance when α is around 0.3, while smaller values like $\alpha = 0.1$ or larger values like $\alpha = 0.7$ can potentially degrade the model performance. In Figs. 5.4c, d, when using a user-item matrix with 20% density, the optimal value of α is also around 0.3 for MAE and around 0.6 for RMSE. The optimal values of MAE and RMSE are different since MAR and RMSE are different metrics following different evaluation criteria. As in Figs. 5.4a–d, the

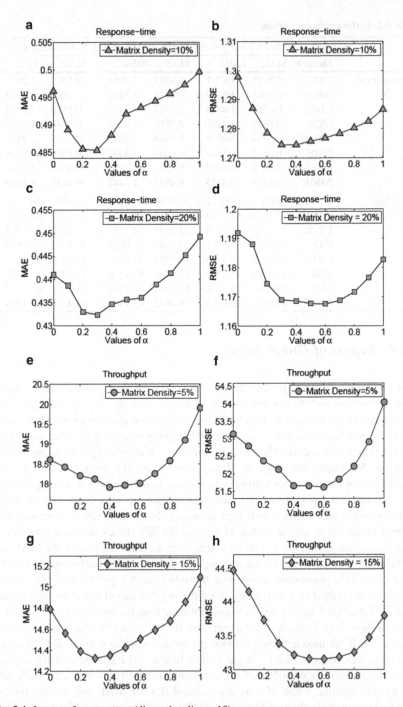

Fig. 5.4 Impact of parameter α (dimensionality $= 10$)

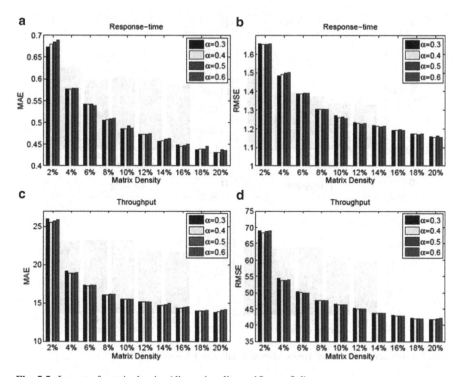

Fig. 5.5 Impact of matrix density (dimensionality $= 10$, $\alpha = 0.4$)

optimal α values of Figs. 5.4e–h are all between 0.3 and 0.6. This observation indicates that optimally combining the two methods can achieve better prediction accuracy than purely or heavily relying on one kind of method, and this is why we used $\alpha = 0.4$ as the default setting in other experiments. As in Table 5.2, another observation from Fig. 5.4 is that a denser matrix provides better prediction accuracy.

5.3.5 Impact of Matrix Density

As shown in Table 5.2 and Fig. 5.4, the prediction accuracy of our NIMF method is influenced by the matrix density. To study the impact of the matrix density on the prediction results, we changed the matrix density from 2 to 20% with a step value of 2%. We set Top-K $= 10$, dimensionality $= 10$, and $\alpha = 0.4$ in this experiment.

Figure 5.5 shows the experimental results, where Figs. 5.5a, b are the experimental results of response time, and Figs. 5.5c, d are the experimental results of throughput. Figure 5.5 shows that when the matrix density is increased from 2 to 4%, the prediction accuracy of the NIMF method is significantly enhanced. With the further increase in matrix density, the speed of prediction accuracy enhancement

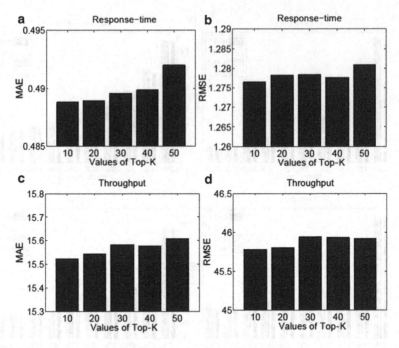

Fig. 5.6 Impact of parameter Top-K (dimensionality = 10, $\alpha = 0.4$)

slows down. This observation indicates that when the matrix is very sparse, the prediction accuracy can be greatly enhanced by collecting more QoS values to make the matrix denser.

5.3.6   Impact of Top-K

The Top-K value determines the number of similar users employed in our NIMF method. To study the impact of the Top-K values on the prediction results, we varied the values of Top-K from 10 to 50 with a step value of 10. We set dimensionality = 10, $\alpha = 0.4$, and matrix density = 10 in this experiment.

Figures 5.6a, b show the MAE and RMSE results of the response time, while Figs. 5.6c, d show the MAE and RMSE results of throughput. Figure 5.6 shows that the MAE and RMSE values slightly increase (prediction accuracy decrease) when the Top-K value is increased from 10 to 50. This is because too large a Top-K value will introduce noise (dissimilar users), which will potentially hurt the prediction accuracy. In all the four figures from Figs. 5.6a–d, the Top-K value of 10 obtains the best prediction accuracy, and this is why we used Top-K = 10 as the default experimental settings in other experiments.

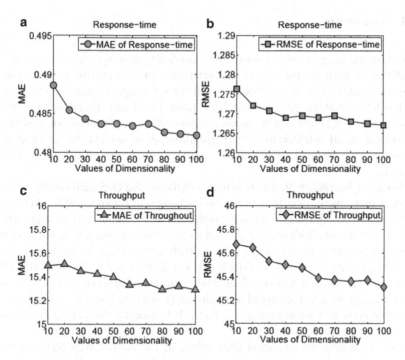

Fig. 5.7 Impact of dimensionality ($\alpha = 0.4$, matrix density $= 10\%$)

5.3.7   Impact of Dimensionality

Dimensionality determines how many latent factors are used to factorize the user-item matrix. To study the impact of the dimensionality, we vary the values of dimensionality from 10 to 100 with a step value of 10. We set Top-K $= 10$, $\alpha = 0.4$, and matrix density $= 10$ in this experiment.

Figures 5.7a, b show the experimental results of the response time, while Figs. 5.7c, d show the experimental results of throughput. As shown in Fig. 5.7, the values of MAE and RMSE decrease (prediction accuracy increases) when the dimensionality is increased from 10 to 100. These observed results coincide with the intuition that relatively larger values of dimensions generate better recommendation results. However, as discussed in Sect. 5.2.4, larger dimensionality values will require longer computation time. Moreover, the dimensionality cannot be set to a very high value since it will cause the overfitting problem, which will potentially hurt the recommendation quality.

5.4 Summary

Based on the intuition that a user's Web service QoS usage experiences can be predicted by both the user's own characteristics and the past usage experiences of other similar users, we propose a neighborhood-integrated matrix factorization approach for making personalized QoS value prediction. Based on the social wisdom of service users, our approach systematically fuses the neighborhood-based and model-based collaborative filtering approaches to achieve higher prediction accuracy. The extensive experimental analysis shows the effectiveness of our approach.

Since the Internet environment is highly dynamic, the QoS performance of Web services may change over time (e.g., due to changes in network traffic, changes in server workload, updates of software implementation). In our current approach, if the user-contributed Web service QoS values are observed over a long duration, the average QoS performance of the unused Web services can be predicted. Since the average Web service QoS performance is relatively stable, the predicted QoS values by our approach provide valuable information for the service users. By taking advantages of the latest advanced technologies in machine learning, we will design an online version of our algorithm to effectively handle this dynamic QoS changing problem in our future work.

After obtaining the predicted QoS values of the unused Web services, most service users will make invocations to the selected Web services. The QoS values of these Web service invocations contain valuable information for improving the QoS prediction accuracy. We plan to design better incentive mechanisms and automatic approaches to enable real-time sharing of these Web service usage experiences among service users. Moreover, we plan to apply our approach to cloud computing environments, where the Web service QoS value collection becomes easier, since the user applications which invoke the Web services are usually deployed and running on the cloud.

We are currently collecting data on failure probabilities of the real-world Web services, which require a long period of observation and sufficient Web service invocations for accurate value measurements. More experimental studies on the failure probability and other Web service QoS properties will be conducted in our future work.

References

1. Breese JS, Heckerman D, Kadie C (1998) Empirical analysis of predictive algorithms for collaborative filtering. In: Proceedings of the 14th annual conference on uncertainty in artificial Intelligence (UAI'98), Madison, Wisconsin, USA, pp 43–52
2. Herlocker JL, Konstan JA, Borchers A, Riedl J (1999) An algorithmic framework for performing collaborative filtering. In: Proceedings of the 22nd international ACM SIGIR conference on research and development in information retrieval (SIGIR'99), Berkeley, pp 230–237

3. Lee DD, Seung HS (1999) Learning the parts of objects by nonnegative matrix factorization. Nature 401(6755):788–791
4. Lee DD, Seung HS (2000) Algorithms for non-negative matrix factorization. In: Proceedings of the advances in neural information processing systems, Denver, USA, pp 556–562
5. Linden G, Smith B, York J (2003) Amazon.com recommendations: item-to-item collaborative filtering. IEEE Internet Comput 7(1):76–80
6. Ma H, King I, Lyu MR (2007) Effective missing data prediction for collaborative filtering. In: Proceedings of the 30th international ACM SIGIR conference on research and development in information retrieval (SIGIR'07), Amsterdam, pp 39–46
7. Ma H, King I, Lyu MR (2009) Learning to recommend with social trust ensemble. In: Proceedings of the 32nd international ACM SIGIR conference on research and development in information retrieval (SIGIR'09), Boston, pp 203–210
8. Rennie JDM, Srebro N (2005) Fast maximum margin matrix factorization for collaborative prediction. In: Proceedings of the 22nd international conference on machine learning (ICML'05), New York, pp 713–719
9. Resnick P, Iacovou N, Suchak M, Bergstrom P, Riedl J (1994) GroupLens: an open architecture for collaborative filtering of netnews. In: Proceedings of ACM conference on computer supported cooperative work, Chapel Hill, pp 175–186
10. Salakhutdinov R, Mnih A (2007) Probabilistic matrix factorization. In: Proceedings of the advances in neural information processing systems, pp 1257–1264
11. Salakhutdinov R, Mnih A (2008) Bayesian probabilistic matrix factorization using Markov chain Monte Carlo. In: Proceedings of the 25th international conference on machine learning (ICML'08), Helsinki, pp 880–887
12. Sarwar B, Karypis G, Konstan J, Riedl J (2001) Item-based collaborative filtering recommendation algorithms. In: Proceedings of the 10th international conference on World Wide Web (WWW'01). ACM, New York, pp 285–295
13. Shao L, Zhang J, Wei Y, Zhao J, Xie B, Mei H (2007) Personalized QoS prediction for Web services via collaborative filtering. In: Proceedings of the 5th international conference on Web services (ICWS'07), Salt Lake City, pp 439–446
14. Zheng Z, Lyu MR (2010) Collaborative reliability prediction for service-oriented systems. In: Proceedings of the IEEE/ACM 32nd international conference on software engineering (ICSE'10). ACM, New York, pp 35–44
15. Zheng Z, Ma H, Lyu MR, King I (2009) WSRec: a collaborative filtering based Web service recommender system. In: Proceedings of the 7th international conference on Web services (ICWS'09), Los Angeles, pp 437–444
16. Zheng Z, Ma H, Lyu MR, King I (2011) QoS-aware Web service recommendation by collaborative filtering. IEEE Trans Serv Comput 4(2):140–152

Chapter 6
Ranking-Based QoS Prediction of Web Services

Abstract The neighborhood-based and model-based collaborative filtering approaches usually try to predict the missing values in the user-item matrix as accurately as possible. However, in the ranking-oriented scenarios, accurate missing value prediction may not lead to accurate ranking. To enable accurate Web service QoS ranking, we propose a ranking-based QoS prediction approach. The contributions of this chapter include the following: (1) identifying the critical problem of personalized quality ranking for Web services and proposing a collaborative QoS-driven quality ranking framework to achieve personalized Web service quality ranking and (2) conducting extensive real-world experiments to study the ranking performance of our proposed algorithm compared with other competing algorithms. The experimental results show the effectiveness of our approach.

Keywords Ranking-based prediction · Quality ranking

6.1 Overview

The neighborhood-based [13, 15] and model-based QoS prediction approaches [14] aim at predicting the Web service QoS values for different service users. These prediction approaches are also named rating-based approaches. The predicted QoS values can be employed to rank the target Web services. In some cases (e.g., Web service search, Web service ranking), the users only need the quality ranking of the target Web services instead of the detailed QoS values. Ranking-based QoS prediction approaches aim at predicting the quality ranking of the target Web services instead of the detailed QoS values. The major challenge in making a QoS-driven Web service quality ranking is that the Web service quality ranking of a user cannot be transferred directly to another user, since the user locations are quite different. Personalized Web service quality ranking is therefore required for different service users.

Z. Zheng and M.R. Lyu, *QoS Management of Web Services*, Advanced Topics in
Science and Technology in China, DOI 10.1007/978-3-642-34207-3_6,
© Zhejiang University Press, Hangzhou and Springer-Verlag Berlin Heidelberg 2013

The most straightforward approach to personalized Web service ranking is to evaluate all the Web services at the user-side and rank the Web services based on the observed QoS performance [4, 7, 10]. However, this approach is impractical in reality since conducting Web services evaluation is time-consuming and resource consuming. Moreover, it is difficult for the service users to evaluate all the Web services themselves since there may exist a huge number of Web services on the Internet.

To attack this critical challenge, we propose a ranking-based QoS prediction framework in this chapter to predict the quality ranking of Web services without requiring additional real-world Web service invocations from the intended user.

The rest of this chapter is organized as follows: Sect. 6.2 describes our collaborative Web service ranking framework. Section 6.3 presents experiments, and Sect. 6.4 concludes the chapter.

6.2   Quality Ranking Framework

This section presents our collaborative Web service quality ranking framework, which is designed as a four-phase process. In phase 1, we calculate the similarity of the users with the current user based on their rankings on the commonly invoked Web services. Then, in phase 2, a set of similar users are identified. After that, in phase 3, a preference function is defined to present the quality priority of two Web services. Finally, in phase 4, a greedy order algorithm is proposed to rank the employed Web services as well as the unemployed Web services based on the preference function and making use of the past usage experiences of other similar users. Details of these phases are presented in Sects. 6.2.1, 6.2.2, 6.2.3, and 6.2.4, respectively.

6.2.1   Ranking Similarity Computation

In our approach, the ranking similarity between users is determined by comparing their personalized Web service quality rankings for the commonly invoked services. Suppose we have a set of three Web services, on which two users have observed response times (seconds) of (1, 2, 4) and (2, 4, 5), respectively. The response-time values on these Web services by the two users are clearly different; nevertheless, their rankings are very close as the Web services are ordered in the same way, based on the response-time values. Given two rankings for the same set of Web services, the Kendall rank correlation coefficient (KRCC) [6] evaluates the degree of similarity by considering the number of inversions of Web service pairs which would be needed to transform one rank order into the other. The KRCC value of user a and user u can be calculated by

$$\text{Sim}(u, v) = \frac{C - D}{N(N - 1)/2},$$ (6.1)

where N is the number of Web services, C is the number of concordant pairs between two lists, and D is the number of discordant pairs. Since $C = N(N - 1)/2 - D$, Eq. (6.1) is equal to $\text{Sim}(u, v) = 1 - \frac{4D}{N(N-1)}$. Employing the Kendall rank correlation coefficient, the similarity between two Web service rankings can be calculated by

$$\text{Sim}(u, v) = 1 - \frac{4 \times \sum\limits_{i,j \in I_u \cap I_v} \tilde{I}\left(\left(q_{u,i} - q_{u,j}\right)\left(q_{v,i} - q_{v,j}\right)\right)}{|I_u \cap I_v| \times (|I_u \cap I_v| - 1)},$$ (6.2)

where $I_u \cap I_v$ is the subset of Web services commonly invoked by user u and user v, $q_{u,i}$ is the QoS value (e.g., response time and throughput) of Web service i observed by user u, and $\tilde{I}(x)$ is an indicator function defined as

$$\tilde{I}(x) = \begin{cases} 1 & \text{if } x < 0 \\ 0 & \text{otherwise} \end{cases}.$$ (6.3)

From the above definition, the ranking similarity between two rankings, $\text{Sim}(u, v)$, is in the interval of $[-1, 1]$, where -1 is obtained when the order of user u is the exact reverse of user v and 1 is obtained when order of user u is equal to the order of user v. Since KRCC compares Web service pairs, the intersection between two users has to be at least 2 (i.e., $|I_u \cap I_v| \geq 2$) for the similarity computation.

6.2.2 Find Similar Users

By calculating the KRCC similarity values between the current user and other users, the users similar to the current user can be identified. Previous ranking approaches [5, 11] usually employ information of all the users for making ranking prediction for the current user, which may include dissimilar users. However, employing QoS values of dissimilar users will greatly influence the prediction accuracy for the current user. To address this problem, our approach employs only the Top-K similar users for making ranking prediction and excludes the users with negative correlations (negative KRCC values). In our approach, a set of similar users $S(u)$ are identified for the current user u by

$$N(u) = \{v | v \in T_u, \text{Sim}(u, v) > 0, v \neq u\},$$ (6.4)

where T_u is a set of the Top-K similar users to the user u and $\text{Sim}(u, v) > 0$ excludes the dissimilar users with negative KRCC values. The value of $\text{Sim}(u, v)$ in Eq. (6.4) can be calculated by Eq. (6.2).

6.2.3 Preference Function

A user's preference for a pair of Web services can be modeled in the form of $\Psi: I \times I \to R$ [5], where $\Psi(i, j) > 0$ means that the quality of Web service i is higher than Web service j and is thus more preferable for the user and vice versa [5]. The value of the preference function $\Psi(i, j)$ indicates the strength of preference, and a value of zero means that there is no preference between the two Web services. The preference function $\Psi(i, j)$ is antisymmetric, that is, $\Psi(i, j) = -\Psi(j, i)$. We set $\Psi(i, i) = 0$ for all $i \in I$.

Given the user-observed QoS values for two Web services, the preference between these two Web services can be easily derived by comparing the QoS values, where $\Psi(i, j) = q_i - q_j$. To obtain preference information regarding the pairs of Web services that have not been invoked by the current user, the QoS values of similar users $S(u)$ are employed. The basic idea is that the more often the similar users in $S(u)$ observe Web service i as higher quality than Web service j, the stronger the evidence for $\Psi(i, j) > 0$ and $\Psi(j, i) < 0$ for the current user. This leads to the following formula for estimating the value of the preference function $\Psi(i, j)$, where Web service i and Web service j are not explicitly observed by the current user u:

$$\Psi(i, j) = \sum_{v \in N(u)^{ij}} w_v \left(q_{v,i} - q_{v,j} \right), \tag{6.5}$$

where v is a similar user of the current u; $N(u)^{ij}$ is a subset of similar users, who obtain QoS values of both Web service i and j; and w_v is a weight factor which can be calculated by

$$w_v = \frac{Sim(u, v)}{\sum_{v \in N(u)^{ij}} Sim(u, v)}. \tag{6.6}$$

w_v makes sure that a similar user with higher similarity has greater impact on the preference value prediction for the current user u.

From Eqs. (6.5) and (6.6), the preference value between a pair of Web services can be obtained by taking advantage of the past usage experiences of the similar users. Assuming there are n Web services to be ranked and user u already obtains QoS values of a Web services, the total number of Web service pairs that can be derived explicitly is $a(a-1)/2$ and the total number of pairs that needs to be predicted from similar users is $n(n-1)/2 - a(a-1)/2$.

6.2.4 Greedy Order Algorithm

Given a preference function Ψ which assigns a score to every pair of Web services $i, j \in I$, we want to choose a quality ranking of Web services in I that agrees with the pairwise preferences as much as possible. Let ρ be a ranking of Web services in I such that $\rho(i) > \rho(j)$ if and only if i is ranked higher than j in the ranking ρ. We can define a value function $V^{\Psi}(\rho)$ that measures the consistency of the ranking ρ with the preference function as follows:

$$V^{\Psi}(\rho) = \sum_{i,j : \rho(i) > \rho(j)} \Psi(i,j). \qquad (6.7)$$

Our goal is to produce a ranking $\rho*$ that maximizes the above objective value function. One possible approach for solving the Web service ranking problem is to search through the possible rankings and select the optimal ranking $\rho*$ that maximizes the value function defined in Eq. (6.7). However, there are $n!$ possible rankings for n Web services. It is impossible to search all the rankings when the value of n is large. Cohen et al. [3] have shown that finding the optimal ranking $\rho*$ is an NP-complete problem.

To enhance the calculation efficiently, we propose a greedy order algorithm in Algorithm 1 (named as CloudRank) for finding an approximately optimal ranking:

Algorithm 1: Greedy Order Algorithm: CloudRank

Input: an employed Web service set E, a full Web service set I, a preference function Ψ

Output: a Web service ranking $\hat{\rho}$

1 $F=E$;
2 **while** $F\neq 0$ **do**
3    $t=$arg max$_{i\in F}\, qi$;
4    $\rho_e(t)=|E|-|F|+1$
5    $F=F-\{t\}$
6 **end**
7 **foreach** $i\in I$ **do**
8    $\pi(i) = \sum_{j\in I} \Psi(i,j)$
9 **end**
10 $n=|I|$
11 **while** $I\neq 0$ **do**
12    $t=$arg max$_{i\in I}\, \pi(i)$
13    $\hat{\rho}(t)=n-|I|+1$
14    $I=I-\{t\}$
15   **foreach** $i\in I$ **do**
16     $\pi(i)=\pi(i)-\Psi(i,j)$
17   **end**
18 **end**
19 **while** $E\neq 0$ **do**
20    $e=$arg max$_{i\in E}\, \rho_e(i)$;
21   index$=$min$_{i\in E}\, \hat{\rho}(i)$
22    $\hat{\rho}(e)=$index
23    $E=E-\{e\}$
24 **end**

Algorithm 1 includes the following steps:

- Step 1 (lines 1–6): Rank the employed Web services in E based on the observed QoS values. $\rho_e(t)$ stores the ranking, where t is a Web service, and the function $\rho_e(t)$ returns the corresponding order of this Web service. The values of $\rho_e(t)$ are in the range of $[1, |E|]$, where a smaller value indicates higher quality.
- Step 2 (lines 7–9): For each Web service in the full Web service set I, calculate the sum of preference values with all other Web services by $\pi(i) = \sum_{j \in I} \Psi(i, j)$. As introduced in Sect. 6.2.3, $\Psi\ (i,\ i) = 0$. Therefore, including $\Psi(i, i)$ in the calculation does not influence the results. Larger $\pi(i)$ value indicates more Web services are less preferred than i (i.e., $\Psi(i, j) > 0$). In other words, Web service i should be ranked in a higher position.
- Step 3 (lines 10–18): Components are ranked from the highest position to the lowest position by picking the Web service t that has the maximum $\pi(t)$ value. The selected Web service is assigned a rank equal to $n - |I| + 1$ so that it will be ranked above all the other remaining Web services in I. The ranks are in the range of $[1, n]$ where n is the number of Web services and a smaller value indicates higher quality. The selected Web service t is then deleted from I, and the preference sum values $\Psi(i)$ of the remaining Web services are updated to remove the effects of the selected Web service t.
- Step 4 (lines 19–24): Step 3 treats the employed Web services in E and the unemployed Web service in $I - E$ identically which may incorrectly rank the employed Web services. In this step, the initial Web service ranking $\rho(i)$ is updated by correcting the rankings of the employed Web services in E. By replacing the ranking results in ρ_i with the corresponding correct ranking of ρ_e (t), our approach makes sure that the employed Web services in E are correctly ranked.

Algorithm 1 has a time complexity of $O(n^2)$, where n is the number of Web services. Compared with the other greedy algorithm [3], our approach guarantees that the employed Web services are correctly ranked. As will be shown in the experiments, our approach provides better ranking accuracy more consistently than the greedy algorithm in [3].

6.3   Experiments

6.3.1   Dataset Description

We evaluate the ranking algorithms using our WS-DREAM[1] Web service QoS dataset [12]. The WS-DREAM dataset includes QoS performance of about

---

[1]http://www.wsdream.net

1.5 million real-world Web service invocations of 100 publicly available Web services observed by 150 distributed users. The QoS values of the 100 Web services observed by the 150 service users can be presented as a 150×100 user-item matrix, where each entry in the matrix is a vector including values of different QoS properties. In the experiment, the *response-time* and *throughput* QoS values are employed independently to rank the Web services.

6.3.2 Evaluation Metric

To evaluate the Web service ranking performance, we employ the normalized discounted cumulative gain (NDCG) [1] metric, which is a popular metric for evaluating ranked results in information retrieval. Given an ideal descending Web service ranking and a predicted descending Web service ranking, the NDCG performance of the Top-K ranked Web services can be calculated by

$$NDCG_k = \frac{DCG_k}{IDCG_k}, \tag{6.8}$$

where DCG_k and $IDCG_k$ are the discounted cumulative gain (DCG) values of the Top-K Web services of the predicted Web service ranking and ideal Web service ranking, respectively. The value of DCG_p can be calculated by

$$DCG_k = rel_1 + \sum_{i=2}^{k} \frac{rel_i}{\log_2 i}, \tag{6.9}$$

where rel_i is the graded relevance (QoS value) of the Web service at position i in the ranking. The premise of DCG is that a high-quality Web service appearing lower in the ranking list should be penalized as the graded relevance value is reduced logarithmically proportional to the position of the result. The DCG value is accumulated cumulatively from the top of the result list to the bottom with the gain of each result discounted at lower ranks. The ideal rank achieves the highest gain among all different rankings. The $NDCG_k$ value is in the interval of 0.0–1.0, where larger value stands for better ranking accuracy since the predicted ranking is nearer the ideal ranking. The value of p is in the interval of 1 to the number of Web services.

6.3.3 User-Based and Item-Based Models

Before conducting a performance comparison of our approach with other approaches, we first briefly introduce some well-known neighborhood-based collaborative filtering approaches in this section. Assume that there are m users and n Web services and the relationship between users and Web services is denoted by an $m \times n$ user-item matrix. Each entry $q_{a,i}$ in the matrix represents the QoS value of Web service i observed by user a. $q_{a,i} = $ null if user a did not invoke Web service i previously.

Vector similarity (VS) views each user as a vector in a high-dimensional vector space based on his/her QoS values. The cosine of the angle between the two corresponding vectors is used to measure the similarity between user a and user u:

$$\text{Sim}(a, u) = \frac{\sum\limits_{i \in I_a \cap I_u} q_{a,i} q_{u,i}}{\sqrt{\sum\limits_{i \in I_a \cap I_u} q_{a,i}^2 \sum\limits_{i \in I_a \cap I_u} q_{u,i}^2}}, \tag{6.10}$$

where $I_a \cap I_u$ is a set of commonly invoked Web services by both user a and user u and $q_{a,i}$ is the QoS value of Web service i observed by the user a.

The Pearson Correlation Coefficient (PCC), another popular similarity computation approach, employs the following equation to compute the similarity between service user a and service user u based on their commonly invoked Web services:

$$\text{Sim}(a, u) = \frac{\sum\limits_{i \in I_a \cap I_u} (q_{a,i} - \overline{q_a})(q_{u,i} - \overline{q_u})}{\sqrt{\sum\limits_{i \in I_a \cap I_u} (q_{a,i} - \overline{q_a})^2} \sqrt{\sum\limits_{i \in I_a \cap I_u} (q_{u,i} - \overline{q_u})^2}}, \tag{6.11}$$

where $\bar{q}_a$ is the average QoS value of all the Web services invoked by user a.

Employing the similar users, the user-based collaborative filtering approaches [2, 9] predict a missing value $q_{u,i}$ in the matrix by the following equation:

$$q_{u,i} = \overline{q_u} + \frac{\sum_{a \in S(u)} \text{Sim}(a, u)(q_{a,i} - \overline{q_a})}{\sum_{a \in S(u)} \text{Sim}(a, u)}, \tag{6.12}$$

where $\text{Sim}(a, u)$ can be calculated by VS or PCC and $\overline{q_u}$ and $\overline{q_a}$ are the average QoS values of different Web services observed by user u and a, respectively.

Similar to the user-based approaches, Eqs. (6.10) and (6.11) (VS and PCC) can also be employed to calculate the similarity between two items (Web services). The item-based approaches [8] predict the missing value employing the similar items. The user-based and item-based approaches can be combined for making missing value prediction [12]:

$$q_{u,i} = \lambda q_{u,i}^1 + (1 - \lambda) q_{u,i}^2, \tag{6.13}$$

where $q_{u,i}^1$ is predicted by the user-based approach and $q_{u,i}^2$ is predicted by the item-based approach.

These above collaborative filtering approaches are rating oriented since they first predict the missing values in the matrix before making Web service ranking. Different from these rating-oriented approaches, our approach ranks the items directly without predicting the missing values in the matrix.

6.3.4 Performance Comparison

To study the personalized Web service ranking performance, we compare our ranking approach (named as CloudRank) with seven other approaches:

- UVS (user-based collaborative filtering method using vector similarity): This method employs vector similarity for calculating the user similarities and employs similar users for the QoS value prediction.
- UPCC (user-based collaborative filtering method using Pearson Correlation Coefficient): This is a very classical method. It employs PCC for calculating the user similarities and employs similar users for the QoS value prediction [2, 9].
- IVS (item-based collaborative filtering method using vector similarity): This method employs vector similarity for computing the item (Web services) similarity when making QoS value prediction.
- IPCC (item-based collaborative filtering method using Pearson Correlation Coefficient): This method is widely used in industrial companies like Amazon. It employs similar items (Web services) for the QoS value prediction [8].
- UIVS (user-based and item-based collaborative filtering using vector similarity): This method combines the user-based and item-based collaborative filtering approaches and employs the vector similarity for the similarity computation for users and items.
- UIPCC (user-based and item-based collaborative filtering using Pearson Correlation Coefficient): This method combines the user-based and item-based collaborative filtering approaches and employs PCC for the similarity computation [12].
- Greedy: This method is proposed for ranking a set of items, which treats the explicitly rated items and the unrated items equally [3]. It does not guarantee that the explicitly rated items will be ranked correctly.

In the real world, the user-item matrices are usually very sparse since a user usually only employs a small number of Web services. In order to conduct our experiments realistically, we randomly remove entries from the user-item matrix to make the matrix sparser with different density. Matrix density (i.e., proportion of nonzero entries) 10%, for example, means that we randomly select 10% of the QoS entries to predict the quality rankings of the users. The rankings based on the original full matrix are employed as ideal rankings to study the ranking performance. The above seven methods together with our CloudRank method are employed for making quality Web services rankings based on the incomplete information. We set Top-K = 10 in our CloudRank method in the experiments.

Table 6.1 NDCG comparison of response time (larger value indicates better ranking accuracy)

Methods	Matrix density = 10%			Matrix density = 30%			Matrix density = 50%		
	NDCG3	10	100	NDCG3	10	100	NDCG3	10	100
UVS	0.9491	0.9104	0.9514	0.9689	0.9476	0.9726	0.9547	0.9408	0.9663
UPCC	0.9347	0.8968	0.9414	**0.9696**	**0.9489**	**0.9729**	0.9541	0.9417	0.9666
IVS	0.9710	0.9308	0.9637	0.9689	0.9442	0.9690	0.9548	0.9417	0.9661
IPCC	0.9737	**0.9359**	**0.9656**	0.9688	0.9466	0.9702	**0.9588**	**0.9484**	0.9695
UIVS	0.9719	0.9304	0.9639	0.9689	0.9441	0.9696	0.9553	0.9423	0.9663
UIPCC	**0.9730**	0.9354	0.9653	0.9691	0.9477	0.9711	0.9584	0.9482	**0.9695**
Greedy	0.9789	0.9523	0.9755	0.9816	0.9728	0.9860	0.9939	0.9843	0.9921
CloudRank	**0.9792**	**0.9532**	**0.9763**	**0.9854**	**0.9760**	**0.9888**	**0.9959**	**0.9864**	**0.9947**
	0.63%	1.85%	1.11%	1.63%	2.85%	1.63%	3.87%	4.01%	2.60%

Table 6.2 NDCG performance comparison of throughput

Methods	Matrix density = 10%			Matrix density = 30%			Matrix density = 50%		
	NDCG3	10	100	NDCG3	10	100	NDCG3	10	100
UVS	0.8588	0.8644	0.9096	0.9164	0.9075	0.9431	0.9061	0.9165	0.9447
UPCC	0.8473	0.8547	0.9010	0.9173	0.9141	0.9456	0.9152	0.9241	0.9504
IVS	0.8752	0.8778	0.9193	0.9173	0.9112	0.9454	0.9133	0.9288	0.9522
IPCC	0.8731	0.8736	0.9185	0.9163	0.9207	0.9482	**0.9249**	**0.9438**	**0.9603**
UIVS	**0.8793**	**0.8800**	**0.9219**	**0.9184**	0.9100	0.9453	0.9100	0.9236	0.9492
UIPCC	0.8789	0.8772	0.9217	0.9176	**0.9215**	**0.9487**	0.9227	0.9406	0.9583
Greedy	0.8951	0.9002	0.9325	0.9109	0.9274	0.9493	0.9229	0.9411	0.9596
CloudRank	**0.8984**	**0.9020**	**0.9341**	**0.9198**	**0.9351**	**0.9551**	**0.9411**	**0.9528**	**0.9689**
	2.17%	2.49%	1.33%	0.15%	1.48%	0.68%	1.75%	0.95%	0.90%

Detailed investigations of the parameter settings (e.g., Top-K values) will be conducted in Sect. 6.3.5. The experimental results are shown in Tables 6.1 and 6.2.

Tables 6.1 and 6.2 show the NDCG performance of response time and throughput, respectively employing 10, 30, and 50% density user-item matrices. In the second row of the table, NDCG3 indicates that the ranking accuracy of the top 3 items is investigated. The value of NDCG3 can be calculated by Eq. (6.8). The first six methods in the table are rating-oriented methods, while the last two methods are ranking-oriented methods. For each column in the tables, we have highlighted the best performer among all methods and the best performer among all the rating-based methods. The values shown in the bottom row are the performance improvements achieved by the best methods over the best rating-oriented methods.

Tables 6.1 and 6.2 show the following:

- Among all the ranking methods, our CloudRank approach obtains better prediction accuracy (larger NDCG values) for both response time and throughput in all the experimental settings consistently.
- The improvements in NDCG3, NDCG5, and NDCG100 of the best method over the best rating-oriented method are 1.92, 2.27, and 1.38% on average.

- Compared with the Greedy approach, our CloudRank method consistently achieves better ranking performance in NDCG3, NDCG10, and NDCG100. As introduced in Sect. 6.2.4, our CloudRank approach makes sure that the employed Web services are correctly ranked.
- When the density of the user-item matrix is increased from 10 to 50%, the ranking accuracy (NDCG values) is also enhanced since a denser user-item matrix provides more information for the missing value prediction.
- The approaches that combine user-based and item-based approaches (UIVS and UIPCC) outperform the user-based approaches (UVS and UPCC) and item-based approaches (IVS and IPCC) in most experimental settings. This observation indicates that by combining the user-based and item-based approaches, better Web service ranking performance can be achieved.

6.3.5 Impact of Parameters

6.3.5.1 Impact of Top-K

The Top-K value determines the number of similar users employed in our CloudRank method. To study the impact of the parameter Top-K on the ranking results, we vary the values of Top-K from 1 to 10 with a step value of 1. We set matrix density $= 20\%$ in this experiment. Two CloudRank versions are implemented, where the first one employs the *enhanced Top-K algorithm* proposed in Sect. 6.2.2 and the second one employs the *traditional Top-K algorithm* without excluding dissimilar users.

Figures 6.1a, b show the NDCG5 and NDCG100 results of the response time, while Figs. 6.1c, d show the NDCG5 and NDCG100 results of throughput. Figure 6.1 shows that the NDCG performance of the *traditional Top-K algorithm* for both response time and throughput decreases when the Top-K value is increased from 1 to 10. This is because large Top-K value will introduce noise and include dissimilar users, which will hurt the ranking accuracy. In all the four figure parts— Figs. 6.1a–d—our *enhanced Top-K algorithm* obtains stable NDCG performance and outperforms the *traditional Top-K algorithm* consistently.

6.3.5.2 Impact of Matrix Density

The ranking accuracy is influenced by the matrix density. To study the impact of the matrix density on the ranking results, we change the matrix density from 5 to 50% with a step value of 5%. We set Top-K $= 10$ in this experiment. Two ranking-based methods (i.e., CloudRank and Greedy) are compared in this experiment.

Figure 6.2 shows the experimental results, where Figs. 6.2a, b are the NDCG5 and NDCG100 results of response time and Figs. 6.2c, d are the NDCG5 and NDCG100 results of throughput. Figure 6.2 shows that when the matrix density is

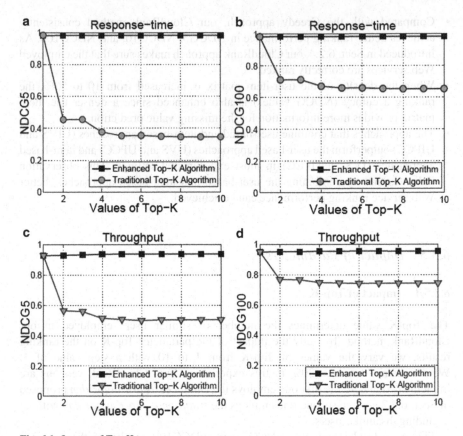

Fig. 6.1 Impact of Top-K

increased from 5 to 50%, the ranking accuracies of both the CloudRank and Greedy methods are significantly enhanced. This observation indicates that the prediction accuracy can be greatly enhanced by collecting more QoS values to make the matrix denser, especially when the matrix is very sparse. In all the four figures parts—Figs. 6.2a–d—our CloudRank method outperforms the Greedy method consistently.

6.4 Summary

In this chapter, we propose a ranking-based QoS prediction framework for Web services. By taking advantage of the past usage experiences of other users, our ranking approach identifies and aggregates the preferences between pairs of Web services to produce a ranking of Web services. We propose a Greedy method for computing the Web service ranking based on the Web service preferences.

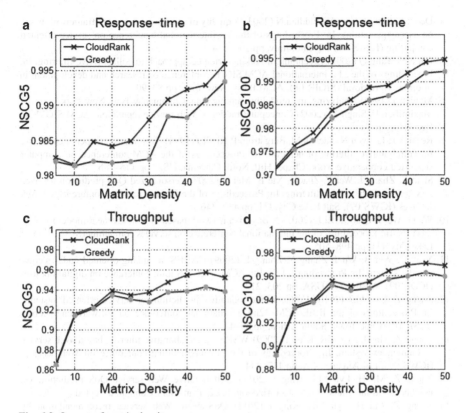

Fig. 6.2 Impact of matrix density

Experimental results show that our approach outperforms the existing rating-based collaborative filtering approaches and the traditional Greedy method.

For future work, we would like to investigate different techniques proposed for improving the ranking accuracy (e.g., data smoothing, random walk, and utilizing content information). We will also conduct more investigations on the correlations and combinations of different QoS properties (our current approach ranks different QoS properties independently).

References

1. Arvelin KJ, Kekalainen J (2002) Cumulated gain-based evaluation of IR techniques. ACM Trans Inf Syst 20(4):422–446
2. Breese JS, Heckerman D, Kadie C (1998) Empirical analysis of predictive algorithms for collaborative filtering. In: Proceedings of the 14th annual conference on uncertainty in artificial intelligence (UAI'98). Morgan Kaufmann Publishers, San Francisco, pp 43–52
3. Cohen WW, Schapire RE, Singer Y (1999) Learning to order things. J Artif Intell Res 10(1):243–270

4. Deora V, Shao J, Gray W, Fiddian N (2003) A quality of service management framework based on user expectations. In: Proceedings of the 1st international conference on service-oriented computing (ICSOC'03), Trento, Italy, pp 104–114
5. Liu NN, Yang Q (2008) Eigenrank: a ranking-oriented approach to collaborative filtering. In: Proceedings of the 31st international ACM SIGIR conference on research and development in information retrieval (SIGIR'08). ACM Press, New York, pp 83–90
6. Marden J (1995) Analyzing and modeling ranking data. Chapman & Hall, New York
7. Maximilien E, Singh M (2002) Conceptual model of Web service reputation. ACM SIGMOD Rec 31(4):36–41
8. Resnick P, Iacovou N, Suchak M, Bergstrom P, Riedl J (1994) GroupLens: an open architecture for collaborative filtering of netnews. In: Proceedings of the ACM conference on computer supported cooperative work, Chapel Hill, North Carolina, USA, pp 175–186
9. Shao L, Zhang J, Wei Y, Zhao J, Xie B, Mei H (2007) Personalized QoS prediction for Web services via collaborative filtering. In: Proceedings of the 5th international conference on Web services (ICWS'07), Salt Lake City, UT, pp 439–446
10. Wu G, Wei J, Qiao X, Li L (2007) A Bayesian network based QoS assessment model for Web services. In: Proceedings of the international conference on services computing (SCC'07), Salt Lake City, UT, pp 498–505
11. Yang C, Wei B, Wu J, Zhang Y, Zhang L (2009) CARES: a ranking-oriented cadal recommender system. In: Proceedings of the 9th ACM/IEEE-CS joint conference on digital libraries (JCDL'09), Austin, TX, USA, pp 203–212
12. Zheng Z, Lyu MR (2010) Collaborative reliability prediction for service-oriented systems. In: Proceedings of the IEEE/ACM 32nd international conference on software engineering (ICSE'10), Cape Town, South Africa, pp 35–44
13. Zheng Z, Ma H, Lyu MR, King I (2009) WSRec: a collaborative filtering based Web service recommender system. In: Proceedings of the 7th international conference on Web services (ICWS'09), Los Angeles, CA, pp 437–444
14. Zheng Z, Ma H, Lyu MR, King I (2011) Collaborative Web service QoS prediction via neighborhood integrated matrix factorization. IEEE Trans Serv Comput, accepted
15. Zheng Z, Ma H, Lyu MR, King I (2011) QoS-aware Web service recommendation by collaborative filtering. IEEE Trans Serv Comput 4(2):140–152

Chapter 7
QoS-Aware Fault Tolerance for Web Services

Abstract The highly dynamic Internet environment makes traditional fault tolerance strategies difficult to be used in the service-oriented environment. In this chapter, we propose an adaptive fault tolerance strategy for Web services, which can determine the optimal fault tolerance strategy dynamically at runtime based on the user preference and service QoS.

Keywords Fault tolerance • User preference • Service QoS

7.1 Overview

The compositional nature of Web services and the unpredictable nature of the Internet pose a new challenge for building reliable SOA systems, which are widely employed in critical domains such as e-commerce and e-government. In contrast to traditional stand-alone systems, an SOA system may break down due to (1) the errors in the SOA system itself, (2) Internet errors (e.g., connection break off, packet loss), and (3) remote Web service problems (e.g., too many users, crashes of the Web services).

There are four technical areas in building reliable software systems, which are fault prevention [11], fault removal [20], fault tolerance [10], and fault forecasting [11]. Since it is difficult to completely remove software faults, software fault tolerance [10] is an essential approach to building highly reliable systems. Critics of software fault tolerance state that developing redundant software components for tolerating faults is too expensive and the reliability improvement is questionable when compared to a single system, considering all the overheads in developing multiple redundant components. In the modern era of service-oriented computing, however, the cost of developing multiple component versions is greatly reduced. This is because the functionally equivalent Web services designed/developed independently by different organizations can be readily employed as redundant alternative components for building diversity-based fault-tolerant systems.

Z. Zheng and M.R. Lyu, *QoS Management of Web Services*, Advanced Topics in Science and Technology in China, DOI 10.1007/978-3-642-34207-3_7,
© Zhejiang University Press, Hangzhou and Springer-Verlag Berlin Heidelberg 2013

A number of fault tolerance strategies for Web services have been proposed in the recent literature [5, 7, 15, 21]. However, most of these strategies are not feasible enough to be applied to various systems with different performance requirements, especially the service-oriented Internet systems in the highly dynamic environment. There is an urgent need for more general and "smarter" fault tolerance strategies, which are context aware and can be dynamically and automatically reconfigured for meeting different user requirements and changing environments. Gaining inspiration from the *user-participation* and *user-collaboration* concepts of Web 2.0, we designed an adaptive fault tolerance strategy and propose a user-collaborative S-aware middleware in making fault tolerance for SOA systems efficient, effective, and optimal.

This chapter aims at advancing the current state-of-the-art of fault tolerance in the field of service reliability engineering. The contributions of this chapter are twofold: (1) We propose a QoS-aware middleware for achieving fault tolerance by employing user participation and user collaboration. By encouraging users to contribute their individually obtained QoS information of the target Web services, more accurate evaluation of the Web services can be achieved, and (2) we propose an adaptive fault tolerance strategy for automatic system reconfiguration at runtime based on the subject user requirements and objective QoS information of the target Web services.

The rest of this chapter is organized as follows: Section 7.2 introduces the QoS-aware middleware design and some basic concepts. Section 7.3 presents various fault tolerance strategies. Section 7.4 designs models for user requirements and QoS. Section 7.5 proposes the adaptive fault tolerance strategy. Section 7.6 presents a number of experiments, and Section 7.7 concludes the chapter.

7.2 QoS-Aware Middleware

In this section, some basic concepts are explained and the architecture of our QoS-aware middleware for fault-tolerant Web services is presented.

7.2.1 Basic Concepts

We divide faults into two types based on the cause of the faults:

- *Network faults:* Network faults are generic to all Web services. For example, *Communication Timeout, Service Unavailable (http 503), Bad Gateway (http 502), Server Error (http 500)*, and so on are network faults. Network faults can be easily identified by the middleware.
- *Logic faults:* Logic faults are specific to different Web services. For example, calculation faults, data faults, and so on are logic faults. Also, various exceptions thrown out by the Web service to the service users are classified into logic-related faults. It is difficult for the middleware to identify such types of faults.

In this chapter, *atomic services* present Web services which provide particular services to users independently. *Atomic services* are self-contained and do not rely on any other Web services. On the other hand, *composite services* present Web services which provide services to users by integrating and calling other Web services [3, 19].

With the popularization of service-oriented computing, various Web services are continuously emerging. The functionalities and interfaces defined by the Web Service Description Language (WSDL) are becoming more and more complex. Machine learning techniques [14, 18] are proposed to identify Web services with similar or identical functionalities automatically. However, the effect and accuracy of these approaches are still far from practical. Since functionally equivalent Web services, which are developed independently by different organizations, may appear with completely different function names, input parameters, and return types, it is really difficult for machines to know that these services are actually providing the same functionalities.

To solve the problem of identical/similar Web service identification, a service community defines a common terminology that is followed by all participants, so that the Web services, which are developed by different organizations, can be described in the same interface [3, 19]. Following a common terminology, automatical Web service composition by programs can be achieved which will attract more users and make the development of the community better.

Companies can enhance their business benefits by joining communities, since a lot of service users will go to the communities to search for suitable services. The coordinator of the community maintains a list of the registered Web services of the community. Before joining the community, a Web service has to follow the interface definition requirements of the community and registers with the community coordinator. In this way, the service community makes sure that various Web services from different organizations in the community come with the same interface.

In this chapter we focus on engaging the Web services in the service communities for fault tolerance and performance enhancement purposes. The design and development of the service communities, which have been discussed in [19], are beyond our scope. We use the word *replica* to represent the functionally equivalent Web services within the same service community.

7.2.2 Middleware Architecture

The architecture of the proposed QoS-aware middleware for fault-tolerant Web services is presented in Fig. 7.1. The work procedure of this middleware is described as follows:

From the Universal Description, Discovery and Integration (UDDI), the middleware obtains the addresses of the service community coordinators.

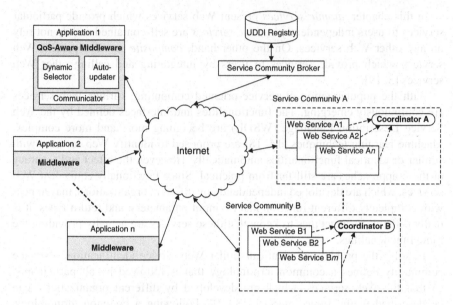

Fig. 7.1 Architecture of the middleware

By contacting the community coordinator, the middleware obtains an address list of the replicas in the community and the overall QoS information of these replicas. The overall QoS information will be used as the initial values in the middleware for optimal fault tolerance strategy configuration. Detailed design of the QoS model of Web services will be introduced in Sect. 7.4.2.

The proposed QoS-aware middleware determines the optimal fault tolerance strategy dynamically based on the user QoS requirements and the QoS information of the target replicas.

The middleware invokes certain replicas with the optimal fault tolerance strategy and records the QoS performance of the invoked replicas.

The middleware dynamically adjusts the optimal fault tolerance strategy based on the overall QoS information and the individually recorded QoS information of the replicas.

As shown in Fig. 7.2, in order to obtain the most up-to-date QoS information of the target replicas for better optimal fault tolerance strategy determination, the middleware will send its individually obtained replica QoS information to the community coordinators in exchange for the newest overall replica QoS information from time to time. By the design of this QoS information exchange mechanism, the community coordinator can obtain replica QoS information from various service users in different geographical locations and use it for providing the overall replica QoS information to the service users.

As shown in Fig. 7.1, the middleware includes the following three parts:

- *Dynamic selector:* In charge of determining the optimal fault tolerance strategy, based on user requirements and the QoS information of replicas dynamically.

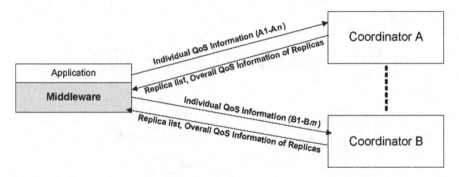

Fig. 7.2 Interaction between the middleware and the coordinators

- *Auto updater:* Updating the newest overall replica QoS information from the community coordinator and providing the obtained QoS information to the coordinator. This mechanism promotes user collaboration to achieve more accurate optimal fault tolerance strategy selection.
- *Communicator:* In charge of invoking certain replicas with the optimal fault tolerance strategy.

7.3 Basic Fault Tolerance Strategies

When applying Web services to critical domains, reliability becomes a major issue. With the popularization of Web services, more and more functionally equivalent Web services are diversely designed and developed by different organizations, making software fault tolerance an attractive choice for service reliability improvement.

There are two major types of fault tolerance strategies: sequential and parallel. *Retry* [5] and *recovery block (RB)* [13] are two major sequential approaches that employ time redundancy to obtain higher reliability. On the other hand, *N-Version Programming (NVP)* [2] and *active* [14] strategies are two major parallel strategies that engage space/resource redundancy for reliability improvement.

In the following, we provide detailed introductions and formula of response time and failure rate for these basic fault tolerance strategies. As discussed in the work [8], we assume that each request is independent and the Web service fails at a fixed rate. Here, we use RTT (round-trip time) to represent the time duration between sending out a request and receiving a response from a service user.

- *Retry:* As shown in Fig. 7.3a, the original Web service will be retried for a certain number of times when it fails. Equation (7.1) is the formula for calculating failure-rate f and RTT t, where m is the number of retries, f_1 is the failure rate of the target Web service, and t_i is the RTT of the ith request:

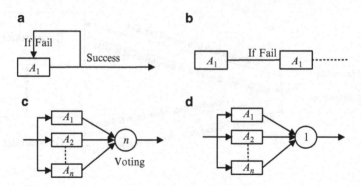

Fig. 7.3 Basic fault tolerance strategies. (**a**) Retry, (**b**) Recovery block, (**c**) NVP, (**d**) Active

$$f = f_1^m; \quad t = \sum_{i=1}^m t_i (f_1)^{i-1}. \tag{7.1}$$

- *RB:* As shown in Fig. 7.3b, another standby Web service (A_2) will be tried sequentially if the primary Web service fails:

$$f = \prod_{i=1}^m f_i; \quad t = \sum_{i=1}^m t_i \prod_{k=1}^{i-1} f_k. \tag{7.2}$$

- *NVP:* As shown in Fig. 7.3c, *NVP* invokes different replicas at the same time and determines the final result by majority voting. It is usually employed to mask logical faults. In Eq. (7.3), n, which is an odd number, represents the total replica number. $F(i)$ represents the failure rate that i ($i \leq n$) replicas fail. For example, assuming $n = 3$, then $f = \sum_{i=2}^3 F(i) = F(2) + F(3) = (1 - f_1) \times f_2 \times f_3 + f_1 \times (1 - f_2) \times f_3 + f_1 \times f_2 \times (1 - f_3) + f_1 \times f_2 \times f_3$:

$$f = \sum_{i=n/2+1}^n F(i); \quad t = \max \left(\{t_i\}_{i=1}^n \right). \tag{7.3}$$

- *Active:* As shown in Fig. 7.3d, *active* strategy invokes different replicas in parallel and takes the first properly returned response as the final result. It is usually employed to mask network faults and to obtain better response-time performance. In Eq. (7.4), Tc is a set of RTTs of the properly returned responses. u is the parallel replica number:

$$f = \prod_{i=1}^u f_i; \quad t = \begin{cases} \min(T_c) : |T_c| > 0 \\ \max(T) : |T_c| = 0 \end{cases}. \tag{7.4}$$

The highly dynamic nature of the Internet and the compositional nature of Web services make the above *static* fault tolerance strategies unpractical in a

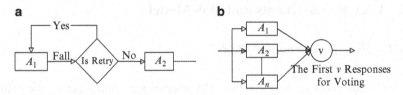

Fig. 7.4 Dynamic fault tolerance strategies. (**a**) Dynamic sequential strategy, (**b**) Dynamic parallel strategy

real-world environment. For example, some replicas may become unavailable permanently, while some new replicas may join in. Moreover, Web service software/hardware may be updated without any notification, and the Internet traffic load and server workload are also changing from time to time. These unpredictable characteristics of Web services provide a challenge for optimal fault tolerance strategy determination. To attack this critical challenge, we propose the following two dynamic fault tolerance strategies, which are more adaptable and can be automatically configured by a QoS-aware middleware in runtime. These two dynamic strategies will be employed in our dynamic fault tolerance strategy selection algorithm in Sect. 7.5.3.

- *Dynamic Sequential Strategy:* As shown in Fig. 7.4a, the dynamic sequential strategy is the combination of *Retry* and *RB* strategies. When the primary replica fails, our algorithm will dynamically determine whether to employ *Retry* or *RB* at runtime based on the QoS of the target replicas and the requirements of service users. The determination algorithm will be introduced in Sect. 7.5.3. In Eq. (7.5), m_i is the number of retries of the ith replica, and n is the total replica quantity. This strategy equals RB when $m_1 = 1$ and equals *Retry* when $m_1 = \infty$:

$$f = \prod_{i=1}^{n} f_i^{m_i}; \quad t = \sum_{i=1}^{n} \left(\left(\sum_{j=1}^{m_i} t_i f_i^{j-1} \right) \prod_{k=1}^{i-1} f_k^{m_i} \right). \tag{7.5}$$

- *Dynamic Parallel Strategy:* As shown in Fig. 7.4b, the dynamic parallel strategy is the combination of *NVP* and *active*. It will invoke u replica at the same time and employ the first v (v is an odd number and $v \le u$) properly returned responses for majority voting. This strategy equals *active* when $v = 1$, and equals *NVP* when $v = u$. Note middle (v, T_c) is employed to calculate the RTT of invoking u replica in parallel and includes the first v for voting, which is equal to the RTT of the vth properly returned response:

$$f = \sum_{i=v/2+1}^{v} F(i); \quad t = \begin{cases} \text{middle}(v, T_c) : |T_c| \ge v \\ \max(T) : |T_c| < v \end{cases}. \tag{7.6}$$

7.4 User Requirements and QoS Model

7.4.1 User Requirement Model

Optimal fault tolerance strategies for SOA systems vary from case to case, which are influenced not only by the QoS of the target replicas but also by the characteristics of the SOA systems. For example, real-time systems may prefer parallel strategies for better response-time performance, while resource-constrained systems (e.g., mobile applications) may prefer sequential strategies for better resource conservation.

It is usually difficult for a middleware to automatically detect the characteristics of an SOA system, such as whether it is latency-sensitive or resource-constrained. The strategy selection accuracy will be greatly enhanced if the service users can provide some concrete requirements/constraints. However, it is impractical and not user-friendly to require the service users, who are often not familiar with fault tolerance strategies, to provide detailed technical information. To address this problem, we designed a simple user requirement model for obtaining necessary requirement information from the users. In this model, the users are required to provide the following four values:

- t_{max}: The largest RTT that the application can afford. t_{max} with a smaller value means a higher requirement on response time, indicating that the application is more latency-sensitive. If the response time of a Web service invocation is larger than t_{max}, the invocation is regarded as *timeout* failure to the service user.
- f_{max}: The largest failure rate that the application can afford. If the failure rate of a Web service is larger than f_{max}, it is not suitable to be employed without fault tolerance strategies.
- r_{max}: The largest resource consumption constraint. The amount of parallel connection is used to approximately quantify the resource consumption, since connecting more Web services in parallel will consume more computing and networking resources. r_{max} with a smaller value indicates that the application is resource-constrained.
- *mode*: The *mode* can be set by the service users to be *sequential, parallel,* or *auto*. *Sequential* means invoking the replicas sequentially (e.g., for the payment-oriented Web services). *Parallel* means that the user prefers invoking the target replicas in parallel. *Auto* means that the users let the middleware determine the optimal mode automatically. We need the service users to provide this *mode* information, because the middleware may not be *smart* enough to detect whether the target replicas are payment-oriented services or not.

The user requirements obtained by this model will be used in our dynamic fault tolerance strategy selection algorithm in Sect. 7.5.3.

7.4.2 Service Community

In addition to the subjective user requirements, the objective QoS information of the target Web service replicas are also needed for the optimal fault tolerance strategy determination. A lot of previous tasks are focused on building the QoS model for Web services [6, 12, 17]. However, there are still several challenges to be solved:

- *It is difficult to obtain performance information of the target Web services.* Service users do not always record the QoS information of the target replicas, such as RTT, failure rate, and so on. Also, most of the service users are unwilling to share the QoS information they obtain.
- *Distributed geographical locations of users make evaluation of target Web services difficult.* Web service performance is influenced by the communication links, which may cause performance evaluation results provided by one user to be inapplicable to others. For example, a user located in the same local area network (LAN) as the target Web service is more likely to yield good performance. The optimistic evaluation result provided by this user may misguide other users who are not in the same LAN as the target Web service.
- *Lack of a convenient mechanism for service users to obtain QoS information of Web services.* QoS information can help service users be aware of the quality of a certain Web service and determine whether to use it or not. However, in reality it is very difficult for the service users to obtain accurate and objective QoS information of the Web services.

To address the above challenges, we designed a QoS model for Web services employing the concept of user participation and user collaboration, which is the key innovation of Web2.0. The basic idea is that by encouraging users to contribute their individually obtained QoS information of the target replicas, we can collect a lot of QoS data from the users located in different geographical locations under various network conditions and engage these data to make the objective overall evaluation of the target Web services.

Based on the concept of service community and the architecture shown in Fig. 7.1, we use the community coordinator to store the overall QoS information of the replicas. Users will periodically send their individually obtained replica QoS information to the service community in exchange for the newest overall replica QoS information, which can be engaged for better optimal strategy determination. Since the middleware will record QoS data of the replicas and exchange it with the coordinator automatically, updated replica QoS information is conveniently available for service users.

For a single replica, the community coordinator will store the following information:

- t_{avg}: The average RTT of the target replica
- t_{std}: The standard deviation of RTT of the target replica
- fl: The logic failure rate of the target replica
- fn: The network failure rate of the target replica

Currently, we only consider the most important QoS properties in our QoS model, which include RTT, logic faults, network faults, and resource consumption. Other QoS properties, however, can be easily included in the future. For those users who are not willing to exchange QoS data with the community coordinator, they can simply close the exchange functionality of the middleware, although this will reduce the dynamic optimal strategy selection performance. This is similar to BitTorrent [4] download, where stopping the uploading of files to others will hurt the download speed of the user.

7.5 Adaptive Fault Tolerance Strategy Configuration

7.5.1 Notations

The notations used in this chapter are listed as follows:

$\{ws_i\}_{i=1}^n$: A set of functionally equivalent replicas

$\{c_{ij}\}_{j=1}^{k+2}$: A set of $(k+2)$ counters for the ws_i

$\{p_{ij}\}_{j=1}^{k+2}$: The probability of an RTT belonging to different categories for ws_i

$\{t_i\}_{i=1}^k$: A set of time values, where t_i is the presentative time of the ith time slot
$$t_i = \frac{t_{\max} \times (i-0.5)}{k}$$

$RTT_v = \{rtt_j\}_{j=1}^v$: A set of RTT values of the v replicas

7.5.2 Scalable RTT Prediction

Accurate RTT prediction is important for the optimal fault tolerance strategy selection. Assuming, for example, that there are in total n replicas $\{ws\}_{i=1}^n$ in the service community, we would like to invoke v ($v \leq n$) replicas in parallel and use the first properly returned response as the final result. The question is then how to find out the optimal set of replicas that will achieve the best RTT performance?

To solve this problem, we need the RTT distributions of all the replicas. In our previous work [21], all the historical RTT results are stored and employed for RTT performance prediction. However, sometimes it is impractical to require the users to store all the past RTT results, which are ever growing and will consume a lot of storage memory. On the other hand, without historical RTT performance information of the replicas, it is extremely difficult to make an accurate prediction. To address this challenge, we propose a scalable RTT prediction algorithm, which scatters the RTT distributions of a replica to reduce the required data storage.

We divide the user required maximum response-time $t_{\max}$, which is provided by the service user, into k time slots. Instead of storing all the detailed historical RTT results, the service user only needs to store $k+2$ distribution counters $\{c_i\}_{i=1}^{k+2}$

for each replica, where c_1–c_k are used to record the numbers of the Web service invocations which fit into the corresponding time slots. c_{k+1} is used to record network-related faults fn, and c_{k+2} is for recording logic-related faults fl. By describing the RTT distribution information with these counters, Eq. (7.7) can be employed to predict the probability that a future Web service invocation belongs to a category where p_1 to p_k are the probabilities that the invocation will fit into the corresponding time slots, p_{k+1} is the probability that a Web service invocation will fail due to network-related faults, and p_{k+2} is the probability that an invocation will fail due to logic-related faults:

$$p_i = \frac{c_i}{\sum_{i=1}^{k+2} c_i}. \tag{7.7}$$

By the above design, we can obtain approximate RTT distribution information of a replica by storing only $k+2$ counters. The values of time-slot number k can be set to be a larger value to obtain more detailed distribution information, making this algorithm scalable.

The approximate RTT distributions of the replicas, which are obtained by the above approach, can be engaged to predict RTT performance of a particular set of replicas $\{ws_i\}_{i=1}^{v}$. We use $\mathrm{rtt}_i == t_j$ to show that an RTT value belongs to the jth time slot. Assuming that the RTT values of future invocations of the selected v replicas are $\mathrm{RTT}_v = \{\mathrm{rtt}_i\}_{i=1}^{v}$, the probability that rtt_i fits into a certain time-slot t_j ($\mathrm{rtt}_i == t_j$) is provided by p_{ij}. For *active* strategy, the problem of predicting RTT performance by invoking a set of replicas at the same time can be formulated as Eq. (7.8), where $\mathrm{rtt}_x = \min (\mathrm{RTT}_v)$ and $\mathrm{RTT}_v = \{\mathrm{rtt}_i\}_{i=1}^{v}$:

$$\tilde{\mathrm{rtt}} = \sum_{i=1}^{k} (p \,(\mathrm{rtt}_x == t_i) \times t_i). \tag{7.8}$$

Equation (7.9) is employed for calculating the value of $p(\mathrm{rtt}_x == t_i)$, which is needed in Eq. (7.8):

$$p(\mathrm{rtt}_x == t_i) = p(\mathrm{rtt}_x \leq t_i) - p\,(\mathrm{rtt}_x \leq t_{i-1}). \tag{7.9}$$

Therefore, the RTT prediction problem becomes the calculation of the values of $p(\mathrm{rtt}_x \leq t_i)$. Equation (7.10) is employed for calculating the value of $p(\mathrm{rtt}_x \leq t_i)$, where $p(\mathrm{rtt}_x \leq t_i)$ is the probability that the RTT value rtt_v of the last Web service ws_v is smaller than t_i, which can be calculated by $p(\mathrm{rtt}_v \leq t_i) = \sum_{k=1}^{i} p_{vk}$. If rtt_v is smaller than t_i, then $\mathrm{rtt}_x = \min(\mathrm{RTT}_v)$ will be smaller than t_i; otherwise, the remaining Web services ws_v– ws_{v-1} will be calculated by the same procedure recursively:

$$p(\mathrm{rtt}_x \leq t_i) = p(\mathrm{rtt}_v \leq t_i) + p(\mathrm{rtt}_v > t_i) \times p(\min (\mathrm{RTT}_{v-1}) \leq t_i). \tag{7.10}$$

By the above calculation, the RTT performance of the *active* strategy, which invokes the given replicas in parallel and employs the first returned response as final result, can be predicted. By changing the $rtt_x = \min (RTT_v)$ to $rtt_x = \max (RTT_v)$, the above calculation procedure can be used to predict the RTT performance of the *NVP* strategy, which needs to wait for all responses of replicas before the majority voting. By changing the $\min (RTT_v)$ to $middle (RTT_v, y)$, which means the RTT value of the yth returned response, the above algorithm can be used to predict the RTT performance of the *dynamic parallel strategy*. For example, in the *dynamic parallel strategy*, if we invoke 6 replicas in parallel and employ the first 3 returned responses for voting, then the RTT performance of the whole strategy is equal to the RTT of the 3rd returned response.

Therefore, to solve the problem proposed in the beginning of this section, we can predict the RTT performance of different replica sets with v replicas from all the n replicas $\{ws\}_{i=1}^{n}$ and select the set with the best RTT performance.

7.5.3 Adaptive Fault Tolerance Strategy

By employing and integrating the user requirement model designed in Sect. 7.4.1, the QoS model of Web services designed in Sect. 7.4.2, and the RTT prediction algorithm designed in Sect. 7.5.2, we propose a dynamic fault tolerance strategy selection algorithm in this section. As shown in Algorithm 2, the whole selection procedure is composed of three parts: sequential or parallel strategies determination, dynamic sequential strategy determination, and dynamic parallel strategy determination. The detailed descriptions of these three subcomponents are presented in the following sections.

Algorithm 2: The Optimal Fault Tolerance Strategy Determination Algorithm

---

    Data: $t_{max}, f_{max}, r_{max}$, QoS of the replicas
    Result: Optimal fault tolerance strategy
1   Sequential or parallel strategy determination;
2   **if** *sequential* **then**
3
$$d = \frac{1}{m} \times \left(\frac{t_{i+1} - t_i}{t_{max}} + \frac{f_{i+1} - f_i}{f_{max}} \right);$$
4   **if** $d > e$ **then**
5 | Retry;
6   **else**
7 | RB (try another replica);
8   **end**
9   **else**
10 | Calculate performance of the parallel strategies with different v values;
11 | Select the strategy with minimize s_i value as optimal strategy;
12   **end**
13   **return** optimal fault tolerance strategy;

7.5.3.1 Sequential or Parallel Strategy Determination

If the value of the attribute *mode* in the user requirement model equals *auto*, we need to conduct sequential or parallel strategy determination based on the QoS performance of the target replicas and the subjective requirements of the users. Equation (7.11) is used to calculate the performance of different strategies, where w_1-w_3 are the user-defined weights for different QoS properties:

$$s_i = w_1 \frac{t_i}{t_{max}} + w_2 \frac{f_i}{f_{max}} + w_3 \frac{r_i}{r_{max}}. \qquad (7.11)$$

The underlying consideration is that the performance of a particular response time is related to the user requirement. For example, 100 ms is a large latency for the latency-sensitive applications, while it may be negligible for non-latency-sensitive applications. By using $\frac{t_i}{t_{max}}$, where t_{max} represents the user requirement of response time, we can have a better representation of the response-time performance for service users with different requirements. Failure-rate f_i and resource consumption r_i are similarly considered.

By employing Eq. (7.11), the performance of sequential strategies and parallel strategies can be computed and compared. For sequential strategies, the value of t_i can be calculated by Eq. (7.5), where the value of f_i can be obtained from the middleware and the value of r_i is 1 (only one replica is invoked at the same time). For parallel strategies, the value of t_i can be estimated by using the RTT prediction algorithm presented in Sect. 7.5.2, where the value of f_i can be obtained from the middleware and the value of r_i is the number of parallel invocation replicas. From the sequential and parallel strategies, the one with smaller s_i value will be selected.

7.5.3.2 Dynamic Sequential Strategy Determination

If the value of the attribute *mode* provided by the service user is equal to *sequential* or the sequential strategy is selected by the above selection procedure conducted by the middleware, we need to determine the detailed sequential strategy dynamically based on the user requirements and the QoS values of replicas. $d = \frac{1}{m} \times \left(\frac{t_{i+1}-t_i}{t_{max}} + \frac{f_{i+1}-f_i}{f_{max}} \right)$ is used to calculate the performance difference between two replicas, where $\frac{1}{m}$ is a degradation factor for the *Retry* strategy and m is the number of retries. When $d > e$, where e is the performance degradation threshold, the performance difference between the two selected replicas is large. Therefore, retrying the original replica is more likely to obtain better performance. By increasing the number of retries m, d will become smaller and smaller, reducing the priority of *Retry* strategy and raising the probability that *RB* will be selected.

If the primary replica fails, the above procedure will be repeated until either there is a success or the time expires ($RTT \geq t_{max}$).

7.5.3.3 Dynamic Parallel Strategy Determination

If the value of the attribute *mode* provided by the service user is equal to *parallel* or the parallel strategy is selected by the middleware, we need to determine the optimal parallel replica number n and the NVP number v ($v \leq n$) for the dynamic parallel strategy.

By employing the RTT prediction algorithm presented in Sect. 7.5.2, we can predict the RTT performance of various combinations of the value v and n. The number of all combinations can be calculated by $C_n^v = \frac{n!}{v! \times (n-v)!}$, and the failure rate can be calculated with Eq. (7.6). By employing Eq. (7.11), the performance of different n and v combinations can be calculated and compared. The combination with the minimal p value will be selected and employed as the optimal strategy.

7.6 Experiments

A series of experiments is designed and performed for illustrating the QoS-aware middleware and the dynamic fault tolerance selection algorithm. In the experiments, we compare the performance of our dynamic fault tolerance strategy (denoted as *dynamic*) with the other four traditional fault tolerance strategies *Retry*, *RB*, *NVP*, and *active*.

7.6.1 Experimental Setup

Our experimental system is implemented and deployed with JDK6.0, Eclipse3.3, Axis2.0 [1], and Tomcat6.0. We developed six Web services following an identical interface to simulate replicas in a service community. These replicas are employed for evaluating the performance of various fault tolerance strategies in different situations. The service community coordinator is implemented by *Java Servlet*. The six Web services and the community coordinator are deployed on seven PCs. All PCs have the same configuration: Pentium(R) 4 CPU 2.8 GHz, 1 G RAM, 100 Mbits/s Ethernet card, and a Windows XP operating system. In the experiments, we simulate network-related faults and logic-related faults. All the faults are further divided into permanent faults (service is down permanently) and temporary faults (faults occur randomly). The fault injection techniques are similar to the ones proposed in [9, 16].

In our experimental system, service users, who will invoke the six Web service replicas, are implemented as *Java applications*. We first provide six service users with representative requirement settings as typical examples for investigating performance of different fault tolerance strategies in different situations. The detailed user requirements are shown in Table 7.1. We then study the influence of the parameters of the user requirements and report the experimental results.

Table 7.1 Requirements of service users

Users	t_{max}	f_{max}	r_{max}	Focus
User 1	1,000	0.1	50	RTT
User 2	2,000	0.01	20	RTT, Fail
User 3	4,000	0.03	2	RTT, Fail, Res
User 4	10,000	0.02	1	Res
User 5	15,000	0.005	3	Fail, Res
User 6	20,000	0.0001	80	Fail

Table 7.2 Parameters of experiments

	Parameters	Setting
1	Number of replicas	6
2	Network fault probability	0.01
3	Logic fault probability	0.0025
4	Permanent fault probability	0.05
5	Number of time slots	20
6	Performance degradation threshold ([Trial mode])	2
7	Dynamic degree	20
8	w_1	1/3
9	w_2	1/3
10	w_3	1/3

In the experiments, failures are counted when service users cannot get a proper response. For each service request, if the response time is larger than t_{max}, a *timeout failure* is counted.

Our experimental environment is defined by a set of parameters, which are shown in Table 7.2. The *permanent fault probability* means the probability of permanent faults among all the faults, which includes *network-related faults* and *logic-related faults*. The *performance degradation threshold* is employed by the dynamic strategy selection algorithm, which has been introduced in Sect. 7.5.3. *Dynamic degree* is used to control the QoS changing of replicas in our experimental system, where a larger number means more serious changing of QoS properties.

7.6.2 Studies of the Typical Examples

The experimental results of the six service users employing different types of fault tolerance strategies are shown in Tables 7.3, 7.4, 7.5, 7.6, 7.7, and 7.8. The results include the employed fault tolerance strategy (*Strategies*), the number of all requests (*All*), the average RTT of all requests (*RTT*), the number of failures (*Fail*), the average consumed resources (*Res*), and the overall performance (*Perf*, calculated by Eq. (7.11)). The time unit of RTT is in milliseconds (ms).

In the following, we provide a detailed explanation of the experimental results of service user 1. As shown in Table 7.1, the requirements provided by user 1

Table 7.3 Experimental results of user 1

U	Strategies	All	RTT	Fail	Res	Perf
1	Retry	50,000	420	2,853	1	1.011
	RB	50,000	420	2,808	1	1.002
	NVP	50,000	839	2	5	0.939
	Active	50,000	251	110	6	0.393
	Dynamic	50,000	266	298	2.34	0.372

Table 7.4 Experimental results of user 2

U	Strategies	All	RTT	Fail	Res	Perf
2	Retry	50,000	471	285	1	5.985
	RB	50,000	469	283	1	5.944
	NVP	50,000	855	0	5	0.677
	Active	50,000	253	126	6	2.946
	Dynamic	50,000	395	3	4.03	0.459

Table 7.5 Experimental results of user 3

U	Strategies	All	RTT	Fail	Res	Perf
3	Retry	50,000	458	155	1	0.717
	RB	50,000	457	149	1	0.713
	NVP	50,000	845	1	5	2.712
	Active	50,000	248	138	6	3.154
	Dynamic	50,000	456	141	1	0.708

Table 7.6 Experimental results of user 4

U	Strategies	All	RTT	Fail	Res	Perf
4	Retry	50,000	498	145	1	1.194
	RB	50,000	493	131	1	1.180
	NVP	50,000	868	1	5	5.087
	Active	50,000	251	119	6	6.144
	Dynamic	50,000	494	109	1	1.158

Table 7.7 Experimental results of user 5

U	Strategies	All	RTT	Fail	Res	Perf
5	Retry	50,000	454	115	1	0.823
	RB	50,000	450	121	1	0.847
	NVP	50,000	779	0	5	1.718
	Active	50,000	249	125	6	2.516
	Dynamic	50,000	489	60	1.46	0.759

Table 7.8 Experimental results of user 6

U	Strategies	All	RTT	Fail	Res	Perf
6	Retry	50,000	470	146	1	29.236
	RB	50,000	468	119	1	23.835
	NVP	50,000	839	1	5	0.304
	Active	50,000	249	132	6	26.487
	Dynamic	50,000	473	1	3.56	0.268

are $t_{max} = 1,000$, $f_{max} = 0.1$, and $r_{max} = 50$. These requirement settings indicate that user 1 cares more about the response time than the failure rate and resources, because 1,000 ms maximal response-time setting is tight in the highly dynamic Internet environment, and the settings of the failure rate and the resource consumption are loose. As shown in Table 7.3, among all the strategies, the RTT performance of the *NVP* strategy is the worst since it needs to wait for all parallel responses before voting; the RTT performance of the *active* strategy is the best, since it employs the first properly returned response as the final result. The *dynamic* strategy can provide good RTT performance, which is near the performance of the *active* strategy.

The *Fail* column in Table 7.3 shows the fault tolerance performance of different strategies. The failure rates of the *Retry* and *RB* strategies are not good, because these strategies are sequential and the setting of $t_{max} = 1,000$ ms leads to a lot of timeout failures. Among all the strategies, *NVP* obtains the best fault tolerance performance. This is not only because *NVP* can tolerate logic-related faults by majority voting but also because *NVP* invokes five replicas in parallel in our experiments, which greatly reduces the number of *timeout* failures. For example, if one replica does not respond within the required time period t_{max}, *NVP* can still get the correct result by conducting majority voting using the remaining responses. The fault tolerance performance of the *dynamic* strategy is not good compared with *NVP*. However, this fault tolerance performance is already good enough for user 1, who does not care so much about the failure rate by setting $f_{max} = 0.1$.

The *Res* column in Table 7.3 shows the resource consumption information of different fault tolerance strategies. We can see that the resource consumption of *Retry* and *RB* strategies is equal to 1, because these two strategies invoke only one replica at the same time. In our experiments, the version number of *NVP* strategy is set to be 5, and the parallel invocation number of *active* strategy is set to be 6. Therefore, the *Res* of these two strategies are 5 and 6, respectively. The *dynamic* strategy invokes 2.34 replicas in parallel on average. The *Perf* column shows the overall performance of different strategies calculated by Eq. (7.11). We can see that the *dynamic* strategy achieves the best overall performance among all the strategies (smaller value for better performance). Although the *active* strategy also achieves good performance for user 1, in the following experiments, we can see that it cannot always provide good overall performance in different environments.

As shown in Tables 7.4, 7.5, 7.6, 7.7, and 7.8, for other service users the *dynamic* strategy can also provide a suitable strategy dynamically to achieve good performance. As shown in Fig. 7.5, the *dynamic* strategy provides the best overall performance among all the fault tolerance strategies for all the six service users. This is because the *dynamic* strategy considers user requirements and can adjust itself for optimal strategy dynamically according to the change in QoS values of the replicas. The other four traditional fault tolerance strategies perform well in some situations; however, they perform badly in other situations, because they are too static. Our experimental results indicate that the traditional fault tolerance strategies may not be good choices in the field of service-oriented computing, which is highly dynamic. The experimental results also indicate that our proposed *dynamic* fault tolerance strategy is more adaptable and can achieve better overall performance compared with traditional fault tolerance strategies.

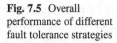

Fig. 7.5 Overall
performance of different
fault tolerance strategies

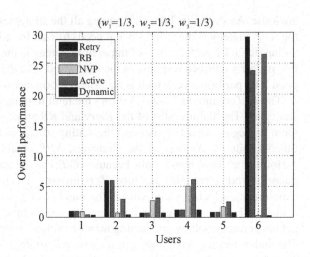

7.6.3   Studies of Different User Requirements

In this section, we conduct experiments with different user requirement settings to study the influence of different requirement parameters (t_{max}, f_{max}, and r_{max}). Each experiment is run 5,000 times, and the experimental results are shown in Fig. 7.6.

Figure 7.6a shows the influence of the user requirement t_{max}, where the x-axis shows the different t_{max} settings (1,000–10,000 ms) and the y-axis is the performance of different fault tolerance strategies calculated by Eq. (7.11). The settings of f_{max} and r_{max} are $f_{max} = 0.1$ and $r_{max} = 6$. Figure 7.6a shows that (1) the performance of the sequential strategies *Retry* and *RB* are worse than the parallel strategies (*NVP* and *active*) when the t_{max} is small (e.g., $t_{max} = 1,000$), since the response-time performance of the sequential strategies are not good; (2) when $t_{max} > 2,000$ ms, sequential fault tolerance strategies achieve better performance than the parallel strategies, since the user requirement for response time is not tight; and (3) the *dynamic* strategy, which is more adaptable, can provide the best performance in all the different t_{max} settings in our experiments.

Figure 7.6b shows the influence of the user requirement f_{max}, where the x-axis shows the different f_{max} settings (0.05–0.5). The settings of t_{max} and r_{max} are $t_{max} = 1,000$ and $r_{max} = 6$. Figure 7.6b shows that (1) the performance of the sequential strategies *Retry* and *RB* are not good when f_{max} is small, since the sequential strategies have a lot of *time out* failures caused by the setting of $t_{max} = 1,000$; (2) the performance of the sequential strategies increases with the increase in f_{max}, since a large f_{max} value indicates that the user requirement for the failure rate is imprecise; (3) parallel strategies can provide steady performance in our experiments; and (4) the *dynamic* strategy can provide the best performance in all the different f_{max} settings.

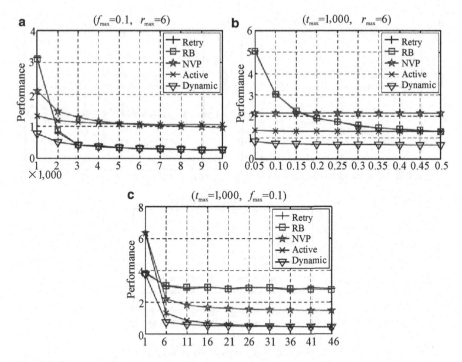

Fig. 7.6 Strategy performance with different t_{max}. (**a**) t_{max}, (**b**) f_{max}, (**c**) r_{max}

Figure 7.6c shows the influence of the user requirement r_{max}, where the x-axis shows different r_{max} settings (1–46). The settings of t_{max} and f_{max} are $t_{max} = 1,000$ and $f_{max} = 0.1$. Figure 7.6c shows that (1) the performance of the parallel strategies is enhanced with an increase in r_{max}, since the user can afford more resource consumption; and (2) the *dynamic* strategy provides the best performance in all the different f_{max} settings.

The above experimental results show that the traditional fault tolerance strategies can provide good performance in some environments. However, with the changing of user requirements, the performance of traditional fault tolerance strategies cannot be guaranteed since these strategies cannot be auto-adapted for different environments. The *dynamic* fault tolerance strategy, on the other hand, provides the best overall performance with different t_{max}, f_{max} and r_{max} settings in our experiments.

7.6.4 Studies of Different Faults

In this section, we study the performance of different fault tolerance strategies with various faults. The user requirements in these experiments are $t_{max} = 2,000$, $f_{max} = 0.1$, $r_{max} = 6$. The experimental results are shown in Fig. 7.7.

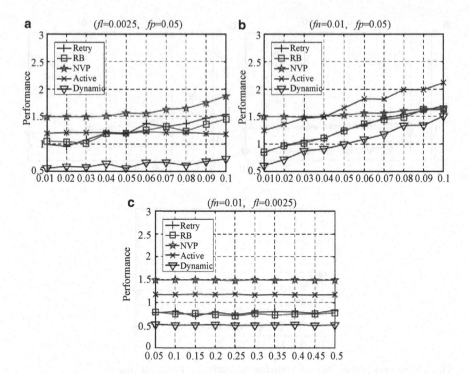

Fig. 7.7 Strategy performance at different levels of faults. (**a**) Network faults (*fn*), (**b**) Logic faults (*fl*), (**c**) Permanent faults (*fp*)

Figure 7.7a shows the performance of different fault tolerance strategies with a different level of network faults (the *x*-axis), which is from 1 to 10%. Figure 7.7a shows that (1) the performance of the *NVP* strategy is not good, since the user requirement of resources is tight ($r_{max} = 6$); (2) the performance of the sequential strategies degrades with the increase in network faults, since more *timeout* errors occur (response time larger than t_{max}); and (3) the *dynamic* strategy can provide the best performance at different levels of network faults.

Figure 7.7b shows the performance of different fault tolerance strategies at different levels of logic faults (1–10%). Figure 7.7(b) shows that (1) with the increase in logic faults, the performance of the *active* strategy degrades, since *active* cannot tolerate logic faults; (2) *NVP* can tolerate logic faults; however, it invokes five replicas in parallel in our experiments, which consumes a lot of resources; and (3) the *dynamic* strategy can provide the best performance at different levels of logic faults.

Figure 7.7c shows the performance of different fault tolerance strategies at different levels of permanent faults (5–50%). Figure 7.7c shows that the *dynamic* strategy can steadily provide the best performance at different levels of permanent faults.

The above experimental results show that the *dynamic* fault tolerance strategy can provide the best overall performance at different levels of network faults, logic faults, and permanent faults.

7.7 Summary

This chapter proposes a QoS-aware adaptive fault tolerance strategy for Web services, which employs both objective replica QoS information as well as subjective user requirements for optimal strategy configuration determination. Based on a QoS-aware middleware, service users share their individually obtained Web service QoS information with each other via a service community coordinator. Experiments are conducted and the performances of various fault tolerance strategies in different environments are compared. The experimental results indicate that the proposed *dynamic* strategy can obtain better overall performance for various service users compared with traditional fault tolerance strategies.

More QoS properties will be involved in our QoS model for Web services in the future. More investigations are needed for the fault tolerance of stateful Web services, which need to maintain states across multiple tasks.

References

1. Apache (2008) Axis2. http://ws.apache.org/axis2
2. Avizienis A (1995) The methodology of N-version programming. In: Lyu MR (ed) Software fault tolerance. Wiley, Chichester, pp 23–46
3. Benatallah B, Dumas M, Sheng QZ, Ngu AHH (2002) Declarative composition and peer-to-peer provisioning of dynamic Web services. In: Proceedings of the 18th international conference on data engineering (ICDE'02), San Jose, CA
4. Bram C (2003) Incentives build robustness in BitTorrent. In: Proceedings of the first workshop economics of peer-to-peer systems, Ann Arbor, Michigan, pp 1–5
5. Chan PP, Lyu MR, Malek M (2007) Reliable Web services: methodology, experiment and modeling. In: Proceedings of the 5th international conference on Web services (ICWS'07), Salt Lake City, UT, pp 679–686
6. Deora V, Shao J, Gray W, Fiddian N (2003) A quality of service management framework based on user expectations. In: Proceedings of the 1st international conference on service-oriented computing (ICSOC'03), Trento, Italy, pp 104–114
7. Foster H, Uchitel S, Magee J, Kramer J (2003) Model-based verification of Web service compositions. In: Proceedings of the 18th IEEE international conference on automated software engineering (ASE'08), L'Aquila, Italy, pp 152–161
8. Leu D, Bastani F, Leiss E (1990) The effect of statically and dynamically replicated components on system reliability. IEEE Trans Reliab 39(2):209–216
9. Looker N, Xu J (2003) Assessing the dependability of SOAP RPC-based Web services by fault injection. In: Proceedings of the 9th international workshop on object-oriented real-time dependable systems, Anacapri, Italy
10. Lyu MR (1995) Software fault tolerance. Trends in software. Wiley, Chichester
11. Lyu MR (1996) Handbook of software reliability engineering. McGraw-Hill, New York

12. Maximilien E, Singh M (2002) Conceptual model of Web service reputation. ACM SIGMOD Rec 31(4):36–41
13. Randell B, Xu J (1995) The evolution of the recovery block concept. In: Lyu MR (ed) Software fault tolerance. Wiley, Chichester, pp 1–21
14. Salatge N, Fabre JC (2007) Fault tolerance connectors for unreliable Web services. In: Proceedings of the 37th international conference on dependable systems and networks (DSN'07), Edinburgh, UK, pp 51–60
15. Tsai W, Paul R, Yu L, Saimi A, Cao Z (2003) Scenario-based Web service testing with distributed agents. IEICE Trans Inf Syst E86-D(10):2130–2144
16. Vieira M, Laranjeiro N, Madeira H (2007) Assessing robustness of Web services infrastructures. In: Proceedings of the 37th international conference on dependable systems and networks (DSN'07), Edinburgh, UK, pp 131–136
17. Wu G, Wei J, Qiao X, Li L (2007) A Bayesian network based QoS assessment model for Web services. In: Proceedings of the international conference on services computing (SCC'07), Salt Lake City, UT, pp 498–505
18. Wu J, Wu Z (2005) Similarity-based Web service matchmaking. In: Proceedings of the international conference on services computing (SCC'05), Orlando, FL, pp 287–294
19. Zeng L, Benatallah B, Ngu AH, Dumas M, Kalagnanam J, Chang H (2004) QoS-aware middleware for Web services composition. IEEE Trans Softw Eng 30(5):311–327
20. Zheng W, Lyu MR, Xie T (2009) Test selection for result inspection via mining predicate rules. In: Companion proceedings of the 31th international conference on software engineering, new ideas and emerging results (ICSE'09), Vancouver, Canada, pp 219–222
21. Zheng Z, Lyu MR (2008) A distributed replication strategy evaluation and selection framework for fault-tolerant Web services. In: Proceedings of the 6th international conference on Web services (ICWS'08), Beijing, China, pp 145–152

Chapter 8
QoS-Aware Selection Framework for Web Services

Abstract This chapter aims at advancing the current state of the art in software fault tolerance for Web services by proposing a systematic and extensible framework. We propose a comprehensive fault tolerance strategy selection framework for systematic design, composition, and evaluation of service-oriented systems. Our framework determines optimal fault tolerance strategy dynamically based on the quality-of-service (QoS) performance of Web services as well as the preferences of service users.

Keywords Fault tolerance • Strategy selection

8.1 Overview

In the service-oriented environment, complex distributed systems can be dynamically composed by discovering and integrating Web services provided by different organizations. As service-oriented architecture (SOA) is becoming a large part of IT infrastructures, building reliable service-oriented systems is more and more important. However, compared with traditional stand-alone software systems, building reliable service-oriented systems is much more challenging, because (1) Web services are usually distributed across the unpredictable Internet, (2) remote Web services are developed and hosted by other providers without any internal design and implementation details, (3) performance of Web services may change frequently (e.g., caused by workload change of servers, internal updates of Web services, performance update of communication links), and (4) the remote Web services may even become unavailable without any advance notification.

An important approach for building reliable systems, software fault tolerance [9] makes the system more robust by masking faults instead of removing faults. One approach of software fault tolerance, also known as *design diversity*, is to employ functionally equivalent yet independently designed components to tolerate faults [9]. Due to the cost of developing redundant components, traditional software

Z. Zheng and M.R. Lyu, *QoS Management of Web Services*, Advanced Topics in
Science and Technology in China, DOI 10.1007/978-3-642-34207-3_8,
© Zhejiang University Press, Hangzhou and Springer-Verlag Berlin Heidelberg 2013

fault tolerance is usually employed only for critical systems. In the area of service-oriented computing [21], however, the cost of developing multiple redundant components is greatly reduced, since the functionally equivalent Web services are provided by different organizations and are accessible via the Internet. These Web services can be employed as alternative components for building diversity-based fault-tolerant service-oriented systems.

A number of fault tolerance strategies have been proposed for Web services in the recent literature, which can be divided into passive replication strategies and active replication strategies. Passive strategies [4, 15, 17] employ a primary service to process the request and invoke another alternative backup service when the primary service fails, while active strategies [8, 11, 13, 14, 16] invoke all the functionally equivalent service candidates in parallel. Complementary to the previous approaches which mainly focus on designing various fault tolerance strategies, we propose a systematic framework for optimal fault tolerance strategy selection, which has never been explored before. Our framework determines optimal fault tolerance strategy dynamically based on the quality-of-service (QoS) performance of Web services as well as the preferences of service users. Moreover, different from the previous approaches which mainly focus on stateless Web services, we apply software fault tolerance strategies for the *stateful Web services*, where multiple tasks have state dependency and must be performed by the same Web services. Moreover, the past research on fault-tolerant Web services [4, 8, 11, 13–17] only considers one single metric (i.e., reliability). This chapter investigates the optimal fault tolerance strategy selection not only by system reliability but also by a lot of other QoS properties (e.g., response time, cost), transactional properties, and user preferences. In our framework, we model the optimal fault tolerance strategy selection problem as an optimization problem, where the user constraints can be expressed by *local constraints* and *global constraints* [22]. By solving the optimization problem, the optimal system fault tolerance configuration can be obtained and dynamical system reconfiguration can be achieved.

This chapter aims at advancing the current state of the art in software fault tolerance for Web services by proposing a systematic and extensible framework. More fault tolerance strategies and more QoS properties can be plugged into our framework easily in the future.

The rest of this chapter is organized as follows: Section 8.2 introduces the motivating example. Section 8.3 presents the system architecture. Section 8.4 proposes selective algorithms for determining optimal fault tolerance strategy. Section 8.5 shows our implementation and experiments, and Sect. 8.6 concludes the chapter.

8.2 Motivating Example

We begin by a motivating example to show the research problems. In this chapter, an *atomic service* is a self-contained Web service which provides service to users independently without relying on any other Web services, a *composite service* represents a Web service which provides service by integrating other Web services, a *stateless*

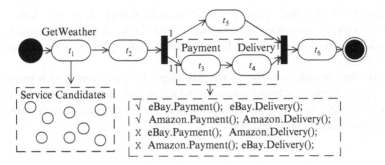

Fig. 8.1 A motivating example

service is a service that does not maintain state information between different invocations (each invocation is independent of the history of client invocations), and a *stateful service* is a service that requires session data maintenance across multiple invocations. A *service plan* is an abstract description of activities for a business process, which is defined as:

Definition 8.1. A service plan *SP* is a triple (T, P, B), where $T = \{t_i\}_{i=1}^{n}$ is a set of tasks, P is a set of settings in the service plan (e.g., execution probabilities of the branches and loops structures), and B provides the structure information of the service plan, which can be specified by XML-based languages, such as BPEL [10].

Figure 8.1 shows a simple service plan which includes six abstract tasks. Each task can be executed by invoking a remote Web service. Following the same assumption of work [1, 2, 19], we assume that for each task in a service plan, there are multiple functionally equivalent Web service candidates that can be adopted to fulfill the task. These functionally equivalent Web services can be obtained from *service communities* [2, 20], which define common terminologies to guarantee that Web services developed by different organizations have the same interface.

For the example shown in Fig. 8.1, there are several challenges to be addressed: (1) There are a number of Web service candidates for the stateless task t_1 (*GetWeather*). Which candidate would be optimal? Does task t_1 require fault tolerance strategy? If so, which fault tolerance strategy is suitable? (2) Assuming that task t_3 (*Payment*) is nonrefundable and task t_4 (*Delivery*) is unreliable, the failure of t_4 (*Delivery*) will lead to inconsistency of the process, since the user has paid the money (cannot be refunded) but cannot get the goods due to delivery failure. How do we detect and avoid such kinds of consistency violations in complex service plans? (3) Task t_3 and t_4 are stateful tasks, which need to maintain states across two invocations. Therefore, it is incorrect to pay one company (e.g., *eBay.Payment* ()) and require another company who did not receive any money to deliver the goods (e.g., *Amazon.Deliver* ()). How to apply fault tolerance strategy for such kinds of stateful tasks? (4) Service users have different preferences and may provide constraints for a single task (named as *local constraints*), such as *response time of t_1 should be less than 1 second*. Service users can also provide constraints for a whole service plan (named as *global constraints*), such as *the execution success* *probability of the whole service plan should be higher than 99%*. Under both the local constraints and global constraints, how do we determine optimal service candidates as well as an optimal fault tolerance strategy for both the stateless and stateful tasks?

This chapter addresses the above challenges by proposing a systematic fault tolerance strategy selection framework, which defines various properties of Web services, identifies commonly used fault tolerance strategies, and designs novel algorithms to attack these challenges.

8.3   System Architecture

Figure 8.2 shows the system architecture of our fault tolerance selection framework for service-oriented systems. Figure 8.2 includes a number of service users, a communication bus (usually the Internet), and a lot of Web services. The execution engines of the service users are in charge of selecting and invoking optimal Web services to fulfill the abstract tasks in the service plans. The execution engine includes several components: *QoS model, fault tolerance strategies, compositional model, consistency checking, and optimal fault tolerance strategy selection*. Details of the first four components will be introduced in Sects. 8.3.1, 8.3.2, 8.3.3, and 8.3.4, respectively, and various optimal fault tolerance strategy selection algorithms will be presented in Sect. 8.4.

The work procedures of our framework are as follows: (1) A service provider obtains the address of a certain service community from the UDDI and registers its Web service in the service community, (2) a service user (usually the developer

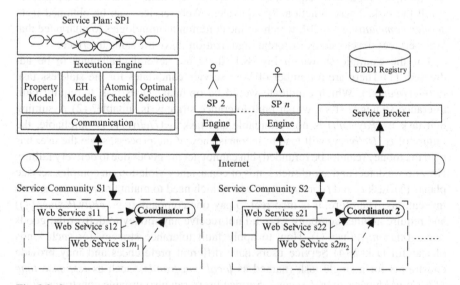

Fig. 8.2 System architecture

Table 8.1 Composition formulas for fault tolerance strategies

QoS Properties	Fault tolerance strategies			
	Retry	RB	NVP	Active
av, sp, osp $(x=1,5,7)$	$1-\left(1-q_1^x\right)^m$	$1-\prod_{i=1}^{m}\left(1-q_i^x\right)$	$\sum_{i=\frac{m}{2}+1}^{m} S^x(i)$	$1-\prod_{i=1}^{m}\left(1-q_i^x\right)$
pr, po, ds $(x=2,3,4)$	$\sum_{i=1}^{m} p_i q_1^x i$	$\sum_{i=1}^{m} p_i\left(\sum_{j=1}^{i} q_j^x\right)$	$\sum_{i=1}^{m} q_i^x$	$\sum_{i=1}^{m} q_i^x$
rt, ort $(x=6,8)$	$\sum_{i=1}^{m} p_i q_1^x i$	$\sum_{i=1}^{m} p_i\left(\sum_{j=1}^{i} q_j^x\right)$	$\max_{i=1}^{m} q_i^x$	$\min_{i=1}^{m} q_i^x$

of SOA systems) designs a service plan, (3) the execution engine obtains a list of candidates with QoS performance for each task in the service plan from the corresponding service communities, (4) the *consistency checking* module checks whether the service plan will cause inconsistency, (5) the *optimal selection* module determines the optimal fault tolerance strategy for the stateless and stateful tasks in the service plan, (6) the execution engine executes the service plan by invoking selected Web services and activates the selected fault tolerance strategy to mask faults, and (7) the execution engine records the QoS performance of the invoked Web services and exchanges this information with the community coordinators for updated QoS information from other service users from time to time.

8.3.1 QoS Properties of Web Services

In the presence of multiple service candidates with identical or similar functionalities, quality of service (QoS) provides nonfunctional characteristics for the optimal candidate selection as well as optimal fault tolerance strategy selection. The most representative QoS properties of Web services include availability, reliability, price, popularity, data size, response time, and failure probability. Given a set of QoS properties, the QoS performance of a Web service can be presented as $q = \left(q^1, \ldots, q^m\right)$, where m is the number of QoS properties.

8.3.2 Fault Tolerance Strategies

To build dependable service-oriented systems, the functionally equivalent service candidates can be employed for tolerating faults [15]. The well-known fault tolerance strategies for Web services are identified in the following, and the formulas for calculating the QoS values of the fault tolerance strategies are listed in Table 8.1.

- *Retry*: The original Web service will be tried a certain number of times if it fails. In Table 8.1, $m(m \geq 2)$ is the maximal execution times of the original Web

Table 8.2 Formulas for basic compositional structures

QoS	Basic compositional structures			
Properties	Sequence	Parallel	Branch	Loop
av, sp, osp ($x = 1, 5, 7$)	$\prod\limits_{i=1}^{n} q_i^x$	$\prod\limits_{i=1}^{n} q_i^x$	$\sum\limits_{i=1}^{n} p_i q_i^x$	$\sum\limits_{i=0}^{n} p_i (q_1^x)^i$
pr, po, ds ($x = 2, 3, 4$)	$\sum\limits_{i=1}^{n} q_i^x$	$\sum\limits_{i=1}^{n} q_i^x$	$\sum\limits_{i=1}^{n} p_i q_i^x$	$\sum\limits_{i=0}^{n} p_i q_1^x i$
rt, ort ($x = 6, 8$)	$\sum\limits_{i=1}^{n} q_i^x$	$\max\limits_{i=1}^{n} q_i^x$	$\sum\limits_{i=1}^{n} p_i q_i^x$	$\sum\limits_{i=0}^{n} p_i q_1^x i$

service. p_i is the probability that the Web service will be executed i times, where the first $i - 1$ executions failed and the ith execution is a success. p_i can be calculated by $p_i = \left(1 - q_1^5\right)^{(i-1)} \times q_1^5$, where q_1^5 is the *success probability* of the original Web service.

- *Recovery Block (RB)*: Another standby service candidate will be invoked sequentially if the primary Web service fails. In Table 8.1, m ($m \leq number$ *of candidates*) is the maximal recovery time, and p_i is the probability that the ith candidate will be executed. p_i can be calculated by $p_i = \left(\prod_{j=1}^{i-1} 1 - q_j^5\right) \times q_i^5$.
- *N-Version Programming (NVP)*: All the m functionally equivalent service candidates are invoked in parallel, and the final result will be determined by majority voting.
- *Active*: All the m service candidates are invoked in parallel, and the first returned response without communication errors will be employed as the final result. *Active* strategy can be employed for improving response-time performance.

Using the formulas in Table 8.1, the aggregated QoS values of different fault tolerance strategies can be calculated. The QoS properties are divided into three groups in Table 8.1 based on their own features. For example, for the *active* strategy, the aggregated QoS values of *price* (q^2), *popularity* (q^3), and *data size* (q^4) are the value sum of its parallel Web services, while the aggregated QoS values of *response time* (q^6) and *overall response time* (q^8) are the minimum values of its parallel Web services.

8.3.3 Service Composition Model

Atomic services can be aggregated by different compositional structures (i.e., sequence, branch, loop, and parallel) which describe the order in which a collection of tasks is executed. These basic compositional structures are included in BPMN [12] and BPEL [10]. The QoS values of the composite services using these structures can be calculated by the formulas in Table 8.2. In the *branch* structure, $\{p_i\}_{i=1}^{n}$ is a set of branch execution probabilities, where $\sum_{i=1}^{n} p_i = 1$. In the *loop* structure, $\{p_i\}_{i=0}^{n}$ is a set of probabilities for executing the loop i times, where n is

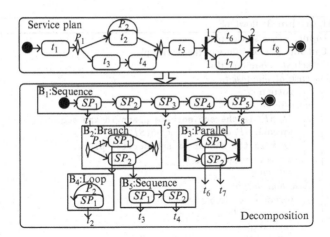

Fig. 8.3 Example of service plan decomposition

the maximum loop time and $\sum_{i=0}^{n} p_i = 1$. In the *parallel* structure, the *response time (rt)* is the maximum value of the n parallel branches, and the *parallel* structure is counted as a success if, and only if, all the n branches succeed.

The basic structures can be nested and combined in arbitrary ways. For calculating the aggregated QoS values of a service plan, we decompose the service plan to basic structures hierarchically. Like the example shown in Fig. 8.3, a service plan is decomposed into basic compositional structures, which will employ the formulas in Table 8.2 to calculate the aggregated QoS values. Algorithm 3 is designed to decompose a service plan into different sub-plans and to calculate the aggregated QoS values hierarchically.

The QoS values of the sub-plans can be stored for reducing the recalculation time when QoS performance of some tasks in the service plan is updated. For example, when the QoS values of t_3 in Fig. 8.3 are updated, we only need to recalculate the QoS values of the blocks B_5, B_2, and B_1. The QoS values of B_3 and B_4 do not need recalculation, since their values remain the same. This design will greatly speed up the QoS recalculation, especially when the task QoS values are updated frequently.

8.3.4 Consistency Checking

To detect inconsistency problems in complex service plans, we propose two transactional properties for the tasks in the service plans.

- *Compensable*: A task is compensable if its effects can be undone after committing to it. In case the overhead or cost of compensating the task is unacceptable, the task is non-compensable. For example, a *payment* task is non-compensable if it is nonrefundable.

Algorithm 3: flowQoS

Input: SP: a service plan
Output: q: QoS values of the service plan

```
1  switch structure type do
2      case atomic task t_i
3      |     return q_i;
4      case sequence
              // SP_i is the sub service plans in the sequence.
5      |     foreach SP_i do q_i = flowQoS(SP_i);
              // k is the number of sub service plans.
6      |     q = sequence(q_1, ..., q_k);
7      |     return q;
8      case branch-split
9      |     foreach SP_i do q_i = flowQoS(SP_i);
10     |     q = branch(P_1, q_1, ..., q_k);
11     |     return q;
12     case Parallel-split
13     |     foreach SP_i do q_i = flowQoS(SP_i);
14     |     q = parallel(q_1, ..., q_k);
15     |     return q;
16     case loop-enter
17     |     q_1 = flowQoS(SP_1);
18     |     q = loop(P, q_1);
19     |     return q;
20     end
21  end
```

- *Reliable*: A task is reliable if its execution success probability is higher than a predefined threshold θ.

The compensable and *reliable* transactional properties of a task t_i are presented as $C(t_i)$ and $R(t_i)$, respectively, where $C(t_i) = true$ means the task is compensable and vice versa. Different from the previous approach [5, 18], our *reliable* property is quantified, which makes our consistency checking approach more realistic and practical. In our approach, the service users can present their judgments on whether a task is reliable or not by setting a user-defined threshold θ. Moreover, when a certain fault tolerance strategy is applied to a task, our approach is able to determine whether the task is reliable or not by employing the formulas in Table 8.1 to calculate the aggregated execution success probability of the whole fault tolerance strategy.

Before proposing our consistency checking algorithm, we first simplify a service plan by transforming the *loop* structures to *branch* structures using the *loops peeling* technique [1], where loop iterations are presented as a sequence of branches and each branch condition indicates whether the loop has to continue or has to exit. We then decompose a service plan into different execution routes. An execution route is defined as:

Definition 8.2. Execution route (ER_i) is a sub-service plan ($ER_i \subseteq SP$) which includes only one branch in each *branch* structure. Each execution route has an execution probability $pro(ER_i)$, which is the product of all probabilities of the selected branches in the route.

Each execution route is further decomposed into a set of sequential routes. A sequential route is defined as:

Definition 8.3. Sequential route (SR_i) is a sub-service plan which includes only one branch in each *parallel* structure and only one branch in each *branch* structure of a service plan, $SR_i \subseteq SP$.

In this way, a service plan is decomposed into a set of sequential routes. Each sequential route includes a set of tasks which are executed sequentially. A service plan satisfies consistency checking if, and only if, no unreliable tasks are executed after non-compensable tasks in every sequential route, which is formalized as follows:

Definition 8.4. φ is a predicate of a sequential route. $\varphi (SR_i)$ is true if, and only if, $\neg \exists t_a, t_b \in SR_i : C (t_a) = \text{false} \wedge R (t_b) = \text{false} \wedge b > a$.

The predicate φ is true whenever the sequential route SR_i satisfies the consistency checking, and a service plan satisfies the consistency checking if, and only if, all its sequential routes satisfy the consistency checking. Algorithm 4 is designed to check whether a service plan satisfies the consistency. By the above design, a service designer can discover the consistency violation of a service plan at the design time and improve the design before causing any inconsistency problems.

Algorithm 4: Consistency Checking of a Service Plan

Input: a service plan SP
Output: true or false, and the violation task pairs if false
1 SR = get a set of sequential routes from SP;
2 int routeNumber = $|SR|$;
3 **for** $(i = 1; i \leq routeNumber; i{+}{+})$ **do**
4   **if** $check(SR_i) == false$ **then**
5   **return** false;
6   **end**
7 **end**
8 **return** true;

Function Check(*SequentialRoute* SR_i***)**

1 T = get the tasks from SR_i;
2 int taskNumber = $|T|$;
3 **for** $(i = 1; i \leq taskNumber; i{+}{+})$ **do**
4   **if** $(C(t_i)==true)$ **then**
5   continue;
6   **end**
7   **for** $(j = i + 1; j \leq taskNumber; j{+}{+})$ **do**
8   **if** $(R(t_i)==false)$ **then**
9   print t_i and t_j;
10   **return** false;
11   **end**
12   **end**
13 **end**
14 **return** true;

8.4 Fault Tolerance Strategy Selection

8.4.1 Notations and Utility Function

The notations used in the rest of this chapter are defined in Table 8.3. Given a service plan SP, T is a set of stateless (SLT) and stateful tasks (SET) in SP. For a task t_i, there is a set of candidates S_i. Each candidate s_{ij} has a quality vector $q_{ij} = \left(q_{ij}^k \right)_{k=1}^c$ presenting the nonfunctional QoS characteristics, where c is the number of QoS properties. We assume that values of QoS properties are real numbers in a bounded range with minimum and maximum values, since some QoS properties are positive (a larger value presents higher quality, e.g., *availability* and *popularity*), while some QoS properties are negative (a smaller value presents better quality, e.g., *price* and *response time*). We transform all the positive QoS properties to negative ones using

$$q_{ij}^k = \max q^k - q_{ij}^k \tag{8.1}$$

We then normalize the values of the QoS properties, which have different scales, to be within the interval of [0,1] by employing the Simple Additive Weighting technique [6]

$$q_{ij}^k = \begin{cases} \frac{q_{ij}^k - \min q^k}{\max q^k - \min q^k} & \text{if } \max q^k \neq \min q^k \\ 1 & \text{if } \max q^k = \min q^k \end{cases} \tag{8.2}$$

where $\min q^k$ and $\max q^k$ are the minimum and maximum QoS values of the kth QoS property, respectively.

Table 8.3 Notations of the selection algorithm

Symbol	Description
SP	A service plan, which is a triple (T, P, B)
ER	A set of execution routes of SP, $ER = \{ER_i\}_{i=1}^{n_e}$
$pro\,(E\,R_i)$	The execution probability of ER_i
SR	A set of sequential routes of SP, $SR = \{SR_i\}_{i=1}^{n_s}$
T	A set of tasks in the service plan, $T = SLT \cup SFT$
SLT	A set of stateless tasks, $SLT = \{t_i\}_{i=1}^{n_l}$
SET	A set of stateful tasks, $SET = \{SFT_i\}_{i=n_l}^n$
SET_i	A set of related tasks of the ith stateful task
S_i	A set of candidates for t_i, $S_i = \{s_{ij}\}_{j=1}^{m_i}$
LC_i	Local constraints for task t_i, $LC_i = \{lc_k^i\}_{k=1}^c$
GC	Global constraints for SP, $GC = \{gc^k\}_{k=1}^c$
q_{ij}	A quality vector for s_{ij}, $q_{ij} = \left(q_{ij}^k\right)_{k=1}^c$
θ	User-defined threshold for the reliable property
ρ_i	The optimal candidate index for t_i

By the above transformation, in the rest of this chapter, the value of the kth QoS property of the jth candidate for the ith task is presented by q_{ij}^k, which is in the interval of $[0,1]$, and a smaller value presents better quality. To quantify the performance of a candidate, a utility function is defined as

$$u_{ij} = \text{utility}\left(t_{ij}\right) = \sum_{k=1}^{c} w_k \times q_{ij}^k, \tag{8.3}$$

where u_{ij} is the utility value of the jth candidate of task i and w_k is the user-defined weight of the kth candidate $\left(\sum_{k=1}^{c} w_k = 1\right)$. By setting the values of w_k, the users (usually a developer of the service-oriented systems) can describe the priorities of different QoS properties.

8.4.2 Selection Candidates

For each abstract task in a service plan, there are two types of candidates that can be adopted for implementing the task: (1) atomic services without any fault tolerance strategies and (2) fault tolerance strategies (e.g., *Retry, RB, NVP*, and *active*). In a service plan, a task t_i is *abortable* if it is designed for noncritical purposes and can be aborted if it fails. Abortable tasks require no fault tolerance strategies. Therefore, the candidate set S_i of an abortable task includes only atomic service candidates, while the candidate set for the non-abortable tasks include both atomic service candidates and fault tolerance strategy candidates.

The fault tolerance strategies have a number of variations based on different configurations. For the *Retry* strategy, there are in total $(r-1)e$ variations, where r is the maximal execution time of *Retry* and e is the number of alternative atomic services. For the *RB, NVP*, and *active* strategies, there are $(e-1)$ variations for each, which are a strategy with the top x $(2 \leq x \leq e)$ best performing atomic services. Therefore, the number of candidates for a non-abortable task t_i in a service plan can be calculated by $m_i = atomicService + basicFTStrategies = e + ((r-1)e + 3(e-1))$. In reality, the values of r and e are usually very small, making the total number of candidates acceptable. If there are too many atomic services (the value if e is too large), we can reduce the value of e by only considering a subset of the best performing candidates based on their utility values.

By solving the optimal candidate selection problem, the optimal candidates are selected for the tasks. In case the selection result for a task is an atomic service, it indicates that no fault tolerance strategy is required for this task, which may be because that the task is abortable or the service candidate is already performing well enough. Our selection framework is extensible, where the current candidates can be updated and new candidates (e.g., new atomic services or new fault tolerance strategies) can be added easily in the future without fundamental changes.

8.4.3   Optimal Selection with Local Constraints

Local constraints ($LC_i = \{lc_i^k\}_{k=1}^c$) specify user requirements for a single task t_i in a service plan. For example, the *response time of the task t_i has to be smaller than 1,000 milliseconds* is a local constraint. For each task, there are c local constraints for the c QoS properties, respectively. Since service users may only set a subset of all the local constraints, the untouched local constraints are set to be $+\infty$ by default so that all the candidates meet the constraints. The optimal candidate selection problem for a single stateless task t_i with local constraints can be formulated mathematically as

Problem 1: Minimize $\sum\limits_{j=1}^{m_i} u_{ij} x_{ij}$.

Subject to

- $\sum\limits_{j=1}^{m_i} q_{ij}^k x_{ij} \leq lc_i^k (k = 1, 2, \ldots, c)$.

- $\sum\limits_{j=1}^{m_i} x_{ij} = 1$.

- $x_{ij} \in \{0, 1\}$.

In Problem 1, x_{ij} is set to 1 if the candidate s_{ij} is selected and 0 otherwise, $q_{ij} = \left(q_{ij}^k\right)_{k=1}^c$ is the QoS vector of candidate s_{ij}, u_{ij} is the utility value of the candidate s_{ij} calculated by Eq. (8.3), and $m_i = |S_i|$ is the number of candidates for task t_i.

To solve Problem 1, for a task t_i, we first use the formulas in Table 8.1 to calculate the aggregated QoS values of the fault tolerance strategy candidates. Then the candidates which cannot meet the local constraints are excluded. After that, the utility values of the candidates are calculated by Eq. (8.3). Finally, the candidate s_{ix} with the smallest (best) utility value will be selected as the optimal candidate for t_i by setting $\rho_i = x$, where ρ is the index of the optimal candidate for task t_i.

In a service plan SP, a stateful task SET_i includes a set of state-related tasks, and the optimal candidate selection for a single task is influenced by other state-related tasks. For example, we can assume a stateful task as (1) *Login*, (2) *Buy a book*, (3) *Logout*, and there are two candidates, that is, *Amazon* and *eBay* for this stateful task. If we select optimal candidates for these three state-related tasks independently, the selection results may be (1) *eBay.login()*, (2) *Amazon.buybook()*, and (3) *eBay.logout()*. However, since the state-related tasks need to maintain states across multiple tasks, it is impossible to login in *eBay* and buy books from *Amazon*. Therefore, the optimal candidates for the state-related tasks of a stateful task should be provided by the same provider, such as (1) *Amazon.login()*, (2) *Amazon.buybook()*, and (3) *Amazon.logout()*.

Algorithm 6 is designed to select optimal candidates for a service plan, which includes stateless tasks (*SLT*) as well as stateful tasks (*SET*). Algorithm 6 first selects optimal candidates for the stateless tasks. Then, for each stateful task SET_i, the overall QoS values of the whole service plan with different candidate sets (operations of the same Web service) are calculated by Algorithm 3, and the utility values of the whole service plan with a different candidate set are calculated by Eq. (8.3). Finally, the candidate set which meets all the local constraints with the best utility performance will be selected as the optimal candidate set for SET_i.

Algorithm 6: Optimal Candidate Selection with LC

Input: Service plan SP, local constraints LC, candidates S
Output: Optimal candidate index ρ for SP.
1 $n_l = |SLT|$; $n_f = |SFT|$; $n = n_l + n_f$; $n_i = |SFT_i|$; $m_i = |S_i|$;
2 **for** *($i = 1; i \le n_l$; $i++$)* **do**
3   **for** *($j = 1; j \le m_i$; $j++$)* **do**
4   **if** $\forall x(q_{ij}^x \le lc_i^x)$ **then** $u_{ij} = utility(q_{ij})$;
5   **end**
6   **if** *no candidate meet lc_i* **then** Throw exception;
7   Select u_{ix} which has minimal utility value u_{ij};
8      $\rho_i = x$;
9 **end**
10 **for** *($i = n_l + 1; i \le n$; $i++$)* **do**
11   **for** *($j = 1; j \le m_i$; $j++$)* **do**
12   **if** $\forall x \forall y(q_{iyj}^x \le lc_{iy}^x)$ **then**
13             $q = flowQoS(SP, q_{i1j}, .., q_{in_ij})$;
14             $u_{ij} = utility(q)$;
15   **end**
16   **end**
17   **if** *no candidate meet lc_i* **then** Throw exception;
18   Select u_{ix} which has minimal utility value u_{ij};
19   **forall** *tasks in SFT_i* **do** $\rho_{ik} = x$;
20 **end**

8.4.4   Optimal Selection with Global Constraints

Local constraints require service users to provide detailed constraint settings for individual tasks, which is time consuming and requires good knowledge of the tasks. Moreover, local constraints cannot specify user requirements for the whole service plan, such as *the response time of the whole service plan should be smaller than 5,000 milliseconds*. To address these drawbacks, we employ global constraints $(GC = \{gc\}_{i=1}^c)$ for specifying user constraints for a whole service plan.

As shown in Sect. 8.3.4, a service plan may include multiple execution routes. To ensure that the service plan meets the global constraints, each execution route should meet the global constraints. For determining optimal candidates for a service plan under global constraints, the simplest way is to employ an exhaustive searching approach to calculate utility values of all candidate combinations and select the one which meets all the constraints and with the best utility performance. However, the exhaustive searching approach is impractical when the task number or candidate number is large, since the number of candidate combinations $\prod_{i=1}^n m_i$ is increasing exponentially, where m_i is the candidate number for task t_i and n is the task number in the service plan.

To determine the optimal candidates for a service plan under both global and local constraints, we model the optimal candidate selection problem as a 0-1 Integer Programming (IP) problem in the following:

Problem 2: Minimize

$$\sum_{ER_k \in SP} \text{freq}_k \times \text{utility}\,(ER_k) \tag{8.4}$$

Subject to

$$\forall k, \sum_{i \in ER_k} \sum_{j \in S_i} q_{ij}^y x_{ij} \le gc^y, (y = 2, 3, 4) \tag{8.5}$$

$$\forall k, \sum_{i \in SR_k} \sum_{j \in S_i} q_{ij}^y x_{ij} \le gc^y, (y = 6, 8) \tag{8.6}$$

$$\forall k, \prod_{i \in ER_k} \prod_{j \in S_i} \left(q_{ij}^y\right)^{x_{ij}} \le gc^y, (y = 1, 5, 7) \tag{8.7}$$

$$\forall SFT_i, x_{y_1 j} = x_{y_2 j} = \cdots = x_{y_{n_i} j} \left(t_{y_i} \in SFT_i\right) \tag{8.8}$$

$$\forall i, \sum_{j \in S_i} x_{ij} = 1 \tag{8.9}$$

$$x_{ij} \in \{0, 1\} \tag{8.10}$$

In Problem 2, Eq. (8.4) is the objective function, where $freq_k$ and $utility\,(ER_k)$ are the execution frequency and utility value of the kth execution route, respectively. The detailed definition of $utility\,(ER_k)$ will be introduced in the later part of this section. Equation (8.5) shows the global constraints for the *price, popularity, and data size (q^y, $y = 2$, 3, 4),* where the aggregated QoS values of an execution route are the sum of all tasks within the route. Equation (8.6) shows the global constraints for *response time and overall response time (q^y, $y = 6$, 8),* where the aggregated QoS values of a sequential route are the sum of all tasks within the route. For q^6 and q^8, all sequential routes should meet the global constraints to make sure that every execution of the service plan meets the global constraints. Equation (8.7) shows the global constraints for the *availability, success probability, and overall success probability (q^y, $y = 1, 5, 7$),* where the aggregated QoS values of an execution route are the product of all tasks within the route. In Eq. (8.7), x_{ij} is employed as an indicator. If $x_{ij} = 0$, then $\left(q_{ij}^y\right)^{x_{ij}} = 1$, indicating that the candidate is not selected. Equation (8.8) is employed to ensure that a set of state-related tasks (SET_i) will employ operations of the same Web service (the same candidate index j). Equations (8.9) and (8.10) are employed to ensure that only one candidate will be selected for each task in the service plan, where $x_{ij} = 1$ and $x_{ij} = 0$ indicate that a candidate j is selected and not selected for task i, respectively.

In Integer Programming, the objective function and constraint functions should be linear. Therefore, we need to transform Eq. (8.7) from nonlinear to linear. By applying the logarithm function to Eq. (8.7), we obtain a linear equation

$$\forall k, \sum_{i \in ER_k} \sum_{j \in S_i} x_{ij} \ln\left(q_{ij}^y\right) \leq \ln(gc^y) \, (y = 1, 5, 7) \tag{8.11}$$

The objective function needs to be changed accordingly. We define the execution route utility function in the new objective function as

$$\text{utility}(ER_k) = \sum_{y=1}^{c} w_y \times \tilde{q}_{ER_k}^y, \tag{8.12}$$

where c is the number of QoS properties, w_y is the user-defined weight, and $\tilde{q}_{ER_k}^y$ is the aggregated QoS value of the execution path, which can be calculated by

$$\tilde{q}_{ER_k}^y = \begin{cases} \sum\limits_{i \in ER_i} \sum\limits_{j \in S_i} x_{ij} \ln\left(q_{ij}^y\right), (y = 1, 5, 7) \\ \sum\limits_{i \in ER_k} \sum\limits_{j \in S_i} x_{ij} q_{ij}^y, (y \neq 1, 5, 7) \end{cases}. \tag{8.13}$$

In this way, the optimal fault tolerance strategy selection problem is formulated as a 0-1 IP problem. Using the well-known branch-and-bound algorithm [7], the selection problem can be solved and the optimal candidates can be identified for a service plan.

8.4.5 Heuristic Algorithm FT-HEU

For a service plan, a solution is a set of candidate selection results for the tasks in the service plan. A solution is a *feasible solution* if the selected candidates meet all the corresponding local constraints as well as all the global constraints. Otherwise, it is an *infeasible solution*. The IP problem is NP-complete [3]. The problem solving time increases exponentially with the problem size, which makes runtime reconfiguration impractical for complex service plans. To speed up the selection procedure, we design a heuristic algorithm *FT-HEU* in Algorithm 7, which includes the following steps:

- *Step 1* (line 1): The function *findInitialSol()* is invoked to find an initial solution for the service plan *SP*.
- *Step 2* (lines 2–11): The function *flow QoS()* is employed to get the aggregated QoS values of the initial solution. If the initial solution cannot meet the global constraints (*infeasible*), then the *findExCandidate()* function is invoked to find an exchangeable candidate to improve the solution. If such an exchangeable

candidate cannot be found, then a *FeasibleSolutionNotFound* exception will be thrown to the user. Otherwise, the above candidate-exchanging procedures will be repeated until a feasible solution becomes available.

• *Step 3* (lines 12–15): Iterative improvement of the feasible solution by invoking the *feasibleUpgrade()* function. The final solution will be returned when the values of ρ do not change in the iterations.

Algorithm 7: EH-BABHEU

Input: SP, GC, LC, S
Output: ρ // Optimal candidate indexes for SP
// Find an initial solutions
1 $\rho = \text{findInitSol}(SP, GC, LC, S)$;
// Get aggregated QoS of the solution
2 $q_{all} = flowQoS(SP, q_{1\rho_1}, ..., q_{n\rho_n})$;
// If infeasible, change solution
3 **while** $\exists x(\frac{q_{all}^x}{gc^x} > 1)$ **do**
4 　　$S'=\text{findExCandidate}(SP, GC, LC, S, \rho)$;
5 　　**if** $|S'| == 0$ **then**
6 　　　　**throw exception** FeasibleSolutionNotFound
7 　　**else**
8 　　　　**forall** $s_{xy} \in S'$ **do** $\rho_x = y$;
9 　　**end**
10 　　$q_{all} = flowQoS(SP, \rho_1, ..., \rho_n)$;
11 **end**
// If feasible, upgrade the solution
12 **repeat**
13 　　$\rho=\text{feasibleUpgrade}(SP, GC, LC, S, \rho)$;
14 **until** ρ *do not change* ;
15 **return** ρ;

In the following we provide a detailed introduction of the functions of these steps.

8.4.5.1 Find Initial Solution: *findInitialSol()*

The *Initialization* operation in the *findInitialSol()* function sets the QoS values of all the tasks to be the optimal values (e.g., *response time* to be 0, *availability* to be 1) so that the function *flowQoS()* can be employed for calculating the accumulated QoS values for the selected tasks. For example, when the candidates first two tasks are selected, *flowQoS()* will return accumulated QoS values of the first two tasks, since the values of other unselected tasks are set to be optimal.

For ease of presentation, we present a stateful task (a set of state-related tasks) in the same format as a stateless task. For example, in the *findInitialSol()* function, when a task is a stateful task SET_i, $q_{ij}^x \leq lc_{ij}^x$ means that all the state-related tasks meet their corresponding local constraints, $q_{all} = flowQoS(SP, \rho_1, \ldots, \rho_{i-1}, j)$ means the accumulated QoS values of the service plan are employing the jth candidates for all the related tasks in SFT_i, and $\rho_i = x$ means that the xth candidates are selected for all the state-related tasks of SET_i.

Function findInitSol(SP, GC, LC, S)

---

1 $n=|SLT|+|SFT|$; $m_i=|S_i|$;

2 Initialization;

3 **for** $(i=1; i \leq n; i++)$ **do**

4   **for** $(j=1; j \leq m_i; j++)$ **do**

5          $q_{all} = flowQoS(SP, \rho_1, ..., \rho_{i-1}, j)$;

6      $w_t = \begin{cases} \frac{1}{c} & \text{if } q_{all} = 0 \\ \frac{q_{all}}{gc^t} / \sum_{k=1}^{c} \frac{q_{all}}{gc^k} & \text{if } q_{all} \neq 0 \end{cases}$;

7   **if** $\forall x(q_{ij}^x \leq lc_{ij}^x \&\& q_{all}^x \leq gc^x)$ **then**

8              $\lambda_{ij} = \sum_{t=1}^{c} w_t \frac{q_{all}^t}{gc^t}$;

9   **end**

10   **end**

11      $\lambda_{ix} = \min\{\lambda_{ij}\}$;

12      $\rho_i = x$;

13 **end**

14 **return** ρ;

An *accumulated feasible value* λ_{ij} is defined to quantify the feasibility degree of the jth candidate for the ith task:

$$\lambda_{ij} = \sum_{t=1}^{c} w_t \frac{q_{ac}^t}{gc^t}$$

$$w_t = \begin{cases} \dfrac{1}{c} & \text{if } q_{ac} = 0, \\ \dfrac{q_{ac}^t}{gc^t} / \sum_{k=1}^{c} \dfrac{q_{ac}^k}{gc^k} & \text{if } q_{ac} \neq 0 \end{cases} \qquad (8.14)$$

where q_{ac}^k means the accumulated QoS values of the selected candidates, w_t is the weight for the corresponding QoS property, and a smaller λ_{ij} value means the candidate is more suitable. w_t is calculated based on the accumulated values of different QoS properties. When the value of $\frac{q_{ac}^k}{gc^k}$ is near 1, it means that the QoS property q^k is more *dangerous* and needs more attention (larger w_k). For a task in the service plan, by calculating the λ values of all its candidates, we can determine a suitable candidate for the task as the initial solution.

8.4.5.2   Find Exchange Candidate: *findExCandidate*()

If the initial solution is infeasible, the function *findExCandidate*() will be invoked to find an exchangeable candidate. For an *infeasible solution*, the *infeasible factor*, which is calculated by $\frac{q_{all}^x}{gc^x}$, is employed to quantify the degree of infeasibility of the infeasible solution. The exchangeable candidate should meet the following requirements:

It will decrease the highest *infeasible factor* of the quality properties: $\frac{q_{new}^x}{gc^x} < \frac{q_{old}^x}{gc^x}$, where $\frac{q_{old}^x}{gc^x} = \max\left(\frac{q_{old}^1}{gc^1}, ..., \frac{q_{old}^c}{gc^c}\right)$ and $\frac{q_{old}^x}{gc^x} > 1$.

It will not increase the *infeasible factor* of any other previously infeasible properties;
$\forall y \left(\frac{q^y_{\text{new}}}{gc^y} \leq \frac{q^y_{\text{old}}}{gc^y} \right)$, where $\frac{q^y_{\text{old}}}{gc^y} > 1$ and $y \neq x$.
It will not make any previously feasible quality properties become infeasible;
$\forall y \left(\frac{q^y_{\text{new}}}{gc^y} \leq 1 \right)$, where $\frac{q^y_{\text{old}}}{gc^y} \leq 1$.

Function findExCandidate(SP, GC, LC, S, ρ)

1 n=$|SLT|+|SFT|$; $m_i=|S_i|$; $S' = \{\}$;
2 $q_{\text{old}} = flowQoS(SP, \rho_1, ..., \rho_n)$;
   // the maximum infeasible factor
3 $\frac{q^x_{\text{old}}}{gc^x} = \max(\frac{q^1_{\text{old}}}{gc^1}, ..., \frac{q^c_{\text{old}}}{gc^c})$;
4 **for** *(i=1; i $\leq$ n; i++)* **do**
5   **for** *(j=1; j $\leq$ m$_i$; j++)* **do**
6   **if** *j==ρ_i* **then** Continue;
7   **if** $\exists y(q^y_{ij} > lc^y_{ij})$ **then** Continue;
8      $q_{\text{new}} = flowQoS(SP, \rho_1, .., j, .., \rho_n)$;
9   **if** $(\frac{q^x_{\text{new}}}{gc^x} < \frac{q^x_{\text{old}}}{gc^x})$ *and* $\forall y(\frac{q^y_{\text{new}}}{gc^y} \leq \frac{q^y_{\text{old}}}{gc^y} \&\& y \neq x \&\& \frac{q^y_{\text{old}}}{gc^y} > 1$ *and*
       $\forall y(\frac{q^y_{\text{new}}}{gc^y} \leq 1 \&\& \frac{q^y_{\text{old}}}{gc^y} \leq 1)$ **then**
10       $g_{ij} = \frac{q^x_{i\rho_i} - q^x_{ij}}{gc^x}$;
11   **end**
12   **end**
13 **end**
14 $g_{xy} = \max\{g_{ij}\}$;
15 Add s_{xy} to S';
16 **return** S';

If there is more than one exchangeable candidate which meets the above requirements, we will select the one with the best *infeasible factor improvement*, which can be calculated by

$$g_{ij} = \frac{q^x_{i\rho_i} - q^x_{ij}}{gc^x}, \tag{8.15}$$

where g_{ij} represents the *infeasible factor improvement* by changing the value of ρ_i to j. $q^x_{i\rho_i}$ and q^x_{ij} are the QoS values of the original candidate and the new candidate, respectively. x is the QoS property with maximum *infeasible factor*.

8.4.5.3 Feasible Upgrade: *feasibleUpgrade*()

If the solution is feasible, the *feasibleUpgrade*() function is invoked to iteratively improve the feasible solution. In the function, the *QoS saving* v_{ij} is defined as

$$v_{ij} = \sum_{k=1}^{c} w_k \frac{q^k_{\text{new}} - q^k_{\text{old}}}{gc^k}, \tag{8.16}$$

where w_k is also introduced in Eq. (8.14). *Utility gain* presents the utility value improvement of the new solution compared with the old solution, which can be calculated by utility (q_{old}) − utility (q_{new}).

Function feasibleUpgrade(SP, GC, LC, S, ρ)

1 n=$|SLT|+|SFT|$; $m_i=|S_i|$;

2 $q_{old} = flowQoS(SP, \rho_1, ..., \rho_n)$;

3 u_{old} = utility (q_{old});

4 **for** *(i=1; i ≤ n; i++)* **do**

5   **for** *(j=1; j ≤ m_i; j++)* **do**

6   **if** $j==\rho_i$ **then** Continue;

7   **if** $\exists x(\frac{q^x}{lc_{ij}^x} > 1)$ **then** Continue;

8        $q_{new} = flowQoS(SP, \rho_1, ..j.., \rho_n)$;

9   **if** $\exists x(\frac{q_{new}^x}{gc^x} > 1)$ **then** Continue;

10   u_{ij} = utility (q_{new});

11       $w_t = \begin{cases} \frac{1}{a} & \text{if} \quad q_{old} = 0 \\ \frac{q_{old}^t}{gc^t} / \sum_{t=1}^{c} \frac{q_{old}^t}{gc^t} & \text{if} \quad q_{old} \neq 0 \end{cases}$;

12       $v_{ij} = \sum_{t=1}^{c} w_t \frac{q_{new}^t - q_{old}^t}{gc^t}$;

13   **end**

14 **end**

15 **if** $\exists xy(u_{xy} < u_{old} \&\& v_{xy} < 0 \&\& v_{xy} = \min(v_{ij}))$ **then**

16    $\rho_x = y$;

17 **else if** $\exists xy(u_{xy} < u_{old} \&\& \frac{u_{old}-u_{xy}}{v_{xy}} = \max(\frac{u_{old}-u_{ij}}{v_{ij}}))$ **then**

18    $\rho_x = y$;

19 **end**

20 **return** ρ

The feasible upgrade procedure includes the following steps: (1) If there exists at least one feasible upgrade $(u_{new} < u_{old})$ which provides QoS savings $v_{ij} < 0$, the candidate with maximal QoS savings (minimal v_{ij} value) is chosen for exchanging; and (2) if no feasible upgrade with QoS saving exists, then the candidate with maximal utility gain per QoS saving is selected, which is calculated by $\frac{u_{old}-u_{xy}}{v_{xy}}$.

8.4.5.4   Computational Complexity of FT-HEU

The FT-HEU algorithm has a convergence property, since (1) step 2 never involves any feasible property so as to become infeasible or any infeasible property so as to be more infeasible. (2) For each exchange in step 2, the property with the maximal infeasible factor will be improved, and (3) step 3 always upgrades the utility value of the solution, which cannot cause any infinite looping, since there are only a finite number of feasible solutions.

For calculating the upper bound of the worst-case computational complexity of the FT-HEU algorithm, we assume there are n tasks, m candidates for each task, and c quality properties. In step 1, when finding the initial solution, the computation of λ_{ij} is $O(nm)$. In step 2, finding an exchange candidate requires maximal $n(m-1)$ calculations of the alternative candidates, where each calculation will invoke a function *flowQos* with computation complexity of $O(nc)$. Therefore, the computation complexity is $O(n^2(m-1)c)$ for each exchange. The *findExCandidate()* function will be invoked at most $n(m-1)$ times since there are at most $(m-1)$ upgrades for each task. Therefore, the total computation complexity of step 2 is $O(n^3(m-1)^2c)$.

In step 3, for each upgrade, there are $n(m-1)$ iterations for the alternative candidates. For each iteration, the *flowQos* function with computation complexity $O(nc)$ is invoked. Thus, the computation complexity of each upgrade is $O(n^2)$ $(m-1)c$. Since there are maximal $n(m-1)$ upgrades for the whole service plan, the total computation complexity of step 3 is $O(n^3(m-1)^2c)$. Since step 1, step 2, and step 3 are executed in sequence, the combined complexity of the whole FT-HEU algorithm is $O(n^3(m-1)^2c)$.

8.4.6 Dynamic Reconfiguration

The service-oriented environment is highly dynamic, where the QoS performance of candidates may change unexpectedly due to internal change or workload fluctuations. Moreover, new candidates may become available, and requirements of service users may also update. Dynamic reconfiguration of the optimal fault tolerance strategy makes the system more adaptive to the dynamic environment. The reconfiguration procedures are as follows: (1) The initial optimal fault tolerance strategy is calculated by employing our optimal candidate selection approach; (2) the service-oriented application invokes the remote Web services with the selected fault tolerance strategy and records their observed QoS performance (e.g., *response time, failure rate*) of the invoked Web services; and (3) the service-oriented application reconfigures the optimal candidates for the tasks when the performance of the system is unacceptable, the renewal time is reached, new candidates become available, or the user requirements are updated.

By the above reconfiguration approach, service users can handle the frequent changes of the candidates as well as the user requirements. When a Web service undergoes a major internal upgrade with explicit version number change, it will be treated as a new service candidate. The reconfiguration frequency is application-dependent and controlled by the service users, which can be further investigated but is beyond the scope of this chapter.

8.5 Experiments

In this section, we first illustrate our optimal fault tolerance strategy selection approach by a case study. Then, the computational time and selection accuracy of various selection algorithms are studied extensively.

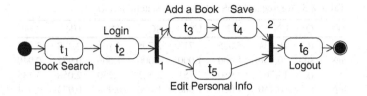

Fig. 8.4 Service plan for case study

Table 8.4 QoS values of the stateless task (t_1)

WS	Q	CN	AU	US	SG	TW	HK	Avg
	rt	3,659	1,218	121	544	934	491	681
aus	sp	0.819	1.000	1.000	1.000	1.000	0.977	0.989
	rt	3,310	1,052	338	472	824	469	686
ajp	sp	0.788	1.000	1.000	1.000	1.000	0.980	0.987
	rt	3,233	1,476	303	596	1,178	612	846
ade	sp	0.813	1.000	1.000	1.000	1.000	0.973	0.987
	rt	3,530	1,190	130	456	916	509	714
aca	sp	0.807	1.000	1.000	1.000	0.998	0.983	0.988
	rt	3,289	1,309	306	600	1,193	630	864
afr	sp	0.844	0.998	1.000	1.000	1.000	0.974	0.989
	rt	3,550	1,326	305	671	1,178	633	862
auk	sp	0.837	0.997	1.000	1.000	1.000	0.971	0.988

8.5.1 Case Study

In this section, we illustrate the optimal fault tolerance strategy selection procedure via a case study: A service user in China (CN) plans to build a simple service-oriented application as shown in Fig. 8.4, where t_1 is a stateless task and t_2–t_6 is a stateful task that includes five state-related tasks. There are six functionally equivalent *Amazon Web services*, which are located in the USA, Japan, Germany, Canada, France, and the UK, respectively, that can be employed for executing the tasks in Fig. 8.4.

Researchers in different geographic locations (NASA@US, CUHK@HK, NTU@SG, SYSU@CN, NTHU@TW, and SUT@AU) are invited to run our WS-DREAM evaluation program for conducting real-world experiments. Benefiting from the *user-collaboration* feature of our Web service evaluation mechanism, the user in *CN* can obtain the Web service QoS information contributed by other service users as shown in Tables 8.4 and 8.5. In these two tables, the *aus*, ..., *auk* in the first column present the six functionally equivalent *Amazon Web services* in different geographic locations. In the first row of the tables, Q presents the QoS properties, *CN*, ..., *HK* present the locations of the service users, and *Avg* presents the *overall response time* (*ort*) and *overall success probability* (*osp*).

Tables 8.4 and 8.5 show that (1) *response-time* performance is greatly influenced by the communication links (e.g., the response-time performance of the user in *US*

Table 8.5 Aggregated QoS values of the stateful task (t_2–t_6)

WS	Q	CN	AU	US	SG	TW	HK	Avg
	rt	16,434	5,625	717	2,708	4,166	2,328	3,297
aus	sp	0.450	1.000	1.000	1.000	1.000	0.972	0.940
	rt	14,763	4,980	1,751	2,505	3,730	2,058	3,335
ajp	sp	0.450	1.000	1.000	1.000	0.998	0.973	0.944
	rt	14,640	6,718	1,646	3,038	5,209	2,730	3,985
ade	sp	0.438	1.000	1.000	1.000	1.000	0.972	0.935
	rt	15,602	5,527	1,403	2,488	4,150	2,305	3,427
aca	sp	0.452	1.000	1.000	1.000	0.996	0.979	0.944
	rt	14,560	5,983	2,211	3,009	5,175	2,862	4,045
afr	sp	0.496	0.992	1.000	1.000	1.000	0.969	0.937
	rt	15,898	6,066	1,630	3,044	5,209	2,819	4,048
auk	sp	0.484	0.988	1.000	1.000	0.998	0.970	0.939

is much better than the user in *CN* in our experiment), (2) optimal service candidates are different from user to user (e.g., *aus* for *US* and *ajp* for *AU*), and (3) invocation *success probabilities* are also different from user to user. In our experiment, the *success probability* of *US* and *SG* is 100%, while the *success probability* of *CN* is less than 85% for the stateless task (t_1) and less than 50% for the stateful task (t_2–t_6). The *success probability* of the stateful task is much lower, since the stateful task is counted as a success only if all the state-related tasks t_2–t_6 are a success. These experimental results show the influence of the unpredictable Internet on the dependability of SOA systems and indicate the necessity of selecting an optimal fault tolerance strategy for different service users based on their observed Web service QoS performance.

To determine the optimal fault tolerance strategy, we set the weights of the eight QoS properties proposed in Sect. 8.3.1 as $(0, 0.2, 0, 0.2, 0.2, 0.2, 0.1, 0.1)$. The weights of q^1 (*availability*) and q^3 (*popularity*) are set to be 0, since the service provider *Amazon* does not provide this information. Since the six *Amazon Web Services* are independent systems and t_2–t_6 are state-related tasks, the optimal candidates for these state-related tasks should be provided by the same Web service. After calculating the candidate utility values, the *FT-BAB* algorithm is employed to determine the optimal candidates for the stateless and stateful tasks. The selection results are as follows: an *active* strategy with the top 2 performing replicas for t_1 and an *active* strategy with 3 parallel branches for the stateful tasks t_2–t_6. This result is reasonable, since the user in *CN* is in a poor network condition in the experiment and the *active* strategy can improve *response-time* performance (by employing the first response as the final result and improve *success probability*) since it fails only if all the replicas fail.

By employing our proposed optimal fault tolerance selection approach, service users can determine optimal fault tolerance strategies for both the stateless and stateful tasks easily. Moreover, the optimal candidates can be easily and dynamically recalculated when the Web service QoS performance is updated.

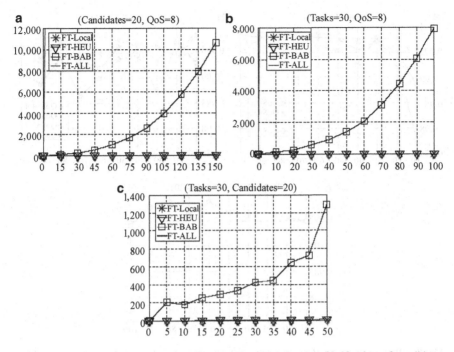

Fig. 8.5 Performance of computation time. (**a**) Number of tasks, (**b**) Number of candidates, (**c**) Number of QoS properties

8.5.2 Performance Study

To study the performance of different selection algorithms (i.e., *FT-Local, FT-ALL, FT-BAB, and FT-HEU*), we randomly select a different number of Web services to create service plans with different compositional structures and execution routes. *FT-Local* is the selection algorithm with local constraints proposed in Algorithm 6, *FT-ALL* represents the exhaustive searching approach introduced in Sect. 8.4.4, *FT-BAB* represents the branch-and-bound algorithm for solving the IP problem, and *FT-HEU* represents the heuristic algorithm shown in Algorithm 7. All the algorithms are implemented in the Java language, and the LP-SOLVE package is employed for the implementation of the *FT-BAB* algorithm. The configurations of the computers for running the experiments are Intel(R) Core(TM)2 2.13 G CPU with 1 G RAM, 100 Mbits/s Ethernet card, Windows XP, and JDK 6.0.

8.5.2.1 Computation Time

Figures 8.5a–c show the computation time performance of different algorithms with a different number of tasks, candidates, and QoS properties, respectively. The experimental result shows (1) the computation time of *FT-ALL* increases

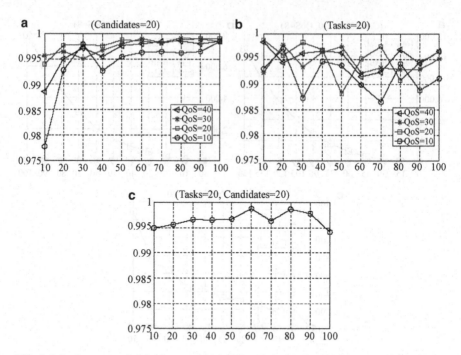

Fig. 8.6 Performance of selection results. (**a**) Number of tasks, (**b**) Number of candidates, (**c**) Number of QoS properties

exponentially even with very small problem size (the curve of *FT-ALL* is almost overlapping the *y*-axis); (2) the computation time of *FT-BAB* is acceptable when the problem size is small; however, it increases quickly when the number of tasks, candidates, and QoS properties is large; (3) the computation time of *FT-HEU* is very small in all the experiments even with large problem size; and (4) the computation time performance of *FT-Local* is the best (near zero); however, *FT-Local* cannot support global constraints.

8.5.2.2   Selection Results

Figure 8.6 compares the selection results of *FT-BAB* and *FT-HEU* algorithms with a different number of tasks, candidates, and QoS properties. The *y*-axis of Fig. 8.6 are the values of *Utility(BAB)/Utility(HEU)*, which are the utility ratios of the two algorithms, where the value of 1 means the selection results by *FT-HEU* are identical to the optimal result obtained by *FT-BAB*.

Figures 8.6a, b show the experimental results of *FT-BAB* and *FT-HEU* with a different number of tasks and candidates, respectively. The experimental results show that (1) with a different number of QoS properties (10, 20, 30, and 40 in the experiment), the utility values of *FT-HEU* are near *FT-BAB* (larger than 0.975

in the experiment) with a different number of tasks and candidates; and (2) with the increase in the task number, the performance of *FT-HEU* becomes better. Figure 8.6c shows the selection result of *FT-BAB* and *FT-HEU* with a different number of QoS properties. The result shows that performance of *FT-HEU* is steady with a different number of QoS properties.

The experimental results show that *FT-HEU* algorithm can provide a near-optimal selection result with excellent computation time performance even with a large problem size. The *FT-HEU* algorithm enables dynamic fault tolerance strategy reconfiguration. *FT-HEU* can be employed in different environments, such as real-time applications (requiring quick response), mobile Web services (with limited computational resources), and large-scale service-oriented systems (with large problem size).

8.6 Summary

In this chapter, we have proposed a fault tolerance strategy selection framework for building dependable service-oriented systems. The main features of this framework are (1) an extensible QoS model of Web services, (2) various fault tolerance strategies, (3) a QoS composition model of Web services, (4) a consistency checking algorithm for complex service plans, and (5) various QoS-aware algorithms for optimal fault tolerance strategy determination for both stateless and stateful Web services.

In this chapter, we employ the average values of historical QoS data for making a selection. More comprehensive investigations will be made of other characteristics of the distributed QoS value, such as standard deviation, worst performance, and moving average. When calculating the aggregated execution success probability, we assume that the failures are independent of each other. More studies will be carried out on the correlative failures of different Web services. Our ongoing research also includes the design of state synchronization mechanisms for alternative stateful Web services and the investigation of more QoS properties of Web services.

References

1. Ardagna D, Pernici B (2007) Adaptive service composition in flexible processes. IEEE Trans Softw Eng 33(6):369–384
2. Benatallah B, Dumas M, Sheng QZ, Ngu AHH (2002) Declarative composition and peer-to-peer provisioning of dynamic Web services. In: Proceedings of the 18th international conference on data engineering (ICDE'02), San Jose, CA
3. Cormen T, Leiserson C, Rivest R (1990) Introduction to algorithms. The MIT Press, Cambridge
4. Fang CL, Liang D, Lin F, Lin CC (2007) Fault-tolerant Web services. J Syst Archit 53(1):21–38
5. Hagen C, Alonso G (2000) Exception handling in workflow management systems. IEEE Trans Softw Eng 26(10):943–958

6. Hwang C-L, Yoon K (1981) Multiple criteria decision making. Lecture notes in economics and mathematical systems. Springer, Berlin

7. Khan S, Manning EG, Li KF, Akbar M (2002) Solving the Knapsack problem for adaptive multimedia systems. Studia Informatica Universalis 2(1):157–178

8. Luckow A, Schnor B (2008) Service replication in Grids: ensuring consistency in a dynamic, failure-prone environment. In: Proceedings of the IEEE International symposium on parallel and distributed processing, Miami, FL, pp 1–7

9. Lyu MR (1995) Software fault tolerance. Trends in software. Wiley, Chichester

10. Ma R, Wu Y, Meng X, Liu S, Pan L (2008) Grid-enabled workflow management system based on BPEL. Int J High Perform Comput Appl 22(3):238–249

11. Merideth MG, Iyengar A, Mikalsen T, Tai S, Rouvellou I, Narasimhan P (2005) Thema: Byzantine fault-tolerant middleware for Web service applications. In: Proceedings of the 24th IEEE symposium on reliable distributed systems (SRDS'05), Orlando, FL, pp 131–142

12. Object Management Group (OMG) (2008) Business process modeling notation version 1.1. URL http://www.omg.org/spec/BPMN/1.1/

13. Pallemulle SL, Thorvaldsson HD, Goldman KJ (2008) Byzantine fault-tolerant Web services for n-tier and service oriented architectures. In: Proceedings of the 28th international conference on distributed computing systems (ICDCS'08), Beijing, China, pp 260–268

14. Salas J, Perez-Sorrosal F, Marta Pati NM, Jiménez-Peris R (2006) WSReplication: a framework for highly available Web services. In: Proceedings of the 15th international conference on World Wide Web (WWW'06), Edinburgh, Scotland, UK, pp 357–366

15. Salatge N, Fabre JC (2007) Fault tolerance connectors for unreliable Web services. In: Proceedings of the 37th international conference on dependable systems and networks (DSN'07), Edinburgh, UK, pp 51–60

16. Santos GT, Lung LC, Montez C (2005) FTWeb: A fault tolerant infrastructure for Web services. In: Proceedings of the 9th IEEE international conference on enterprise computing, Enschede, the Netherlands, pp 95–105

17. Sheu GW, Chang YS, Liang D, Yuan SM, LoW (1997) A fault-tolerant object service on CORBA. In: Proceedings of the 17th international conference on distributed computing systems (ICDCS'97), Baltimore, MA, p 393

18. Ye C, Cheung SC, Chan WK, Xu C (2009) Atomicity analysis of service composition across organizations. IEEE Trans Softw Eng 35(1):2–28

19. Yu T, Zhang Y, Lin KJ (2007) Efficient algorithms for Web services selection with end-to-end QoS constraints. ACM Trans Web 1(1):1–26

20. Zeng L, Benatallah B, Ngu AH, Dumas M, Kalagnanam J, Chang H (2004) QoS-aware middleware for Web services composition. IEEE Trans Softw Eng 30(5):311–327

21. Zhang LJ, Zhang J, Cai H (2007) Services computing. Springer/Tsinghua University Press, Berlin/Beijing

22. Zheng Z, Lyu MR (2009) A QoS-aware fault tolerance middleware for dependable service composition. In: Proceedings of the 39th international conference on dependable systems and networks (DSN'09), Lisbon, Portugal, pp 239–248

Chapter 9
Conclusion and Future Work

Abstract This chapter concludes this book and discusses the future work.

Keywords Web service • QoS management

9.1 Conclusion

The book consists of three parts: The first part deals with Web service QoS evaluation, the second part focuses on Web service QoS prediction, and the third part concentrates on QoS-aware fault-tolerant Web services. All of the approaches proposed in this book are aimed at improving QoS management of Web services.

In the first part, we present a distributed QoS evaluation mechanism for Web services. In order to speed up Web service evaluation, the service users are encouraged to collaborate with each other and share their individually obtained evaluation results. Employing this evaluation mechanism, several real-world Web service evaluations are conducted. The obtained Web service QoS values are released as archival research datasets for other researchers.

In the second part, we propose three QoS prediction approaches for Web services. We first combine the user-based and item-based collaborative filtering approaches to achieve higher prediction accuracy. After that, a neighborhood-integrated model-based approach is proposed. The experimental results show that this model-based approach provides higher prediction accuracy than neighborhood-based approaches. Moreover, this model-based approach is scalable to very large datasets since computation complexity is much less than that of neighborhood-based approaches. Finally, we propose a ranking-based QoS prediction approach for ranking the Web services. Instead of predicting the QoS values, our ranking-based approach predicts the Web service QoS ranking. The experimental results show that the proposed ranking-based approach achieves better prediction accuracy in the ranking scenarios.

In the third part, we conduct two studies of fault-tolerant Web services. We first design an adaptive fault tolerance strategy for Web services, which can be dynamically and automatically updated based on the Web service QoS values as well as the user requirements. After that, we present a systematic and extensible framework for selecting the optimal fault tolerance strategies for Web services. Our selection framework can be employed for both stateless and stateful Web services.

In general, the goal of this book is to evaluate, predict, and use Web service QoS as efficiently and effectively as possible. Our released real-world Web service datasets provide valuable research resources for other researchers.

9.2   Future Work

There are several research directions which require further investigation in the future.

For Web service QoS evaluation, we plan to design more incentive mechanisms to encourage service users to share their observed Web service QoS values. Moreover, since the Web services are highly dynamic, their QoS values may change over time. More investigations are required to study the temporal correlations and periodicity features of Web service QoS values.

For the Web service QoS value prediction, we plan to conduct more research on the correlation and combination of different QoS properties since our current approaches consider different QoS properties independently. Another direction worthy of investigation is exploring the relationship between user information and Web service information since our studies show that combining these two kinds of information generates better prediction accuracy.

For the QoS-aware fault-tolerant Web services, more studies will be carried out on the correlative failures of different Web services since our current approaches assume that failures of different Web services are independent of each other. More research can be conducted on the design of state synchronization mechanisms for the alternative stateful Web services.

Strongly promoted by the leading industrial companies, cloud computing has quickly become popular in recent years. In cloud computing, shared resources, software, and information are provided to computers and other devices on demand, like a public utility. QoS management of cloud computing (e.g., cloud QoS evaluation, prediction, and QoS-aware fault-tolerant cloud) is becoming more and more important. We plan to conduct more studies and extend some of our work to cloud computing.

Zibin Zheng • Michael R. Lyu

QoS Management of Web Services

DOI 10.1007/978-3-642-34207-3_10

This book is a co-publication of Springer and Zhejiang University Press. The ISBN number of the Zhejiang University Press is missing on the copyright page. It should be 978-7-308-10449-4.

Z. Zheng and M.R. Lyu, *QoS Management of Web Services*, Advanced Topics in
Science and Technology in China, DOI 10.1007/978-3-642-34207-3,
© Zhejiang University Press, Hangzhou and Springer-Verlag Berlin Heidelberg 2013

Index

Z. Zheng and M.R. Lyu, *QoS Management of Web Services*, Advanced Topics in
Science and Technology in China, DOI 10.1007/978-3-642-34207-3,
© Zhejiang University Press, Hangzhou and Springer-Verlag Berlin Heidelberg 2013